Discover...

Shakespeare Plays
Series Editor: Klaus Hinz

William Shakespeare: Romeo and Juliet

Teachers' Book

By Norbert Timm and John D. Gallagher

Schöningh Verlag

Norbert Timm: Antworten Akte 1 bis 3, „Reviewing the Play" und
Klausurbeispiel
John D. Gallagher: Antworten Akte 4 und 5 und „Con-Texts"
Sprachliche Betreuung für die Akte 1 bis 3 und andere Teile des
Lehrerbuches: Thomas van Breda

Abbildungen:
S. 28: In: G. Blakemore-Evans, Romeo and Juliet, 1984, S. 31
(Cambridge University Press)
S. 53: AKG

westermann GRUPPE

© 2002 Schöningh Verlag im Westermann Schulbuchverlag GmbH

© ab 2004 Bildungshaus Schulbuchverlage
Westermann Schroedel Diesterweg Schöningh Winklers GmbH
Braunschweig, Paderborn, Darmstadt

www.schoeningh-schulbuch.de
Schöningh Verlag, Jühenplatz 1– 3, 33098 Paderborn

Das Werk und seine Teile sind urheberrechtlich geschützt.
Jede Nutzung in anderen als den gesetzlich zugelassenen Fällen bedarf der
vorherigen schriftlichen Einwilligung des Verlages.
Hinweis zu § 52a UrhG: Weder das Werk noch seine Teile dürfen ohne eine
solche Einwilligung gescannt und in ein Netzwerk gestellt werden.
Dies gilt auch für Intranets von Schulen und sonstigen Bildungseinrichtungen.
Für Verweise (Links) auf Internet-Adressen gilt folgender Haftungshinweis:
Trotz sorgfältiger inhaltlicher Kontrolle wird die Haftung für die Inhalte der
externen Seiten ausgeschlossen. Für den Inhalt dieser externen Seiten sind
ausschließlich deren Betreiber verantwortlich. Sollten Sie daher auf kostenpflichtige,
illegale oder anstößige Inhalte treffen, so bedauern wir dies ausdrücklich und bitten
Sie, uns umgehend per E-Mail davon in Kenntnis zu setzen, damit beim Nachdruck
der Verweis gelöscht wird.

Druck A 8 7 6 / Jahr 2018 17 16
Alle Drucke der Serrie A sind im Unterricht parallel verwendbar.
Die letzte Zahl bezeichnet das Jahr dieses Druckes.

Umschlagentwurf: Veronika Wypior
Druck und Bindung: westermann druck GmbH, Braunschweig

ISBN 978-3-14-040081-7

Inhaltsverzeichnis

	Discover ...: Zielsetzung und methodischer Ansatz	5
Teil I –	Bedeutung der Tragödie „Romeo and Juliet" für Jugendliche	7
Die didaktische	Summary	8
Konzeption	Weiterführende Literatur.	10
	Internet-Adressen.	10
	Filmography	11
Teil II –	Allgemeine Bemerkungen zum methodischen Vorgehen	12
Das Schülerbuch	Anmerkungen zum Prolog im Lehrerhandbuch	14
im Unterricht	**Act One**	16
	Start here	16
	Scene 1	16
	Scene 2	19
	Scene 3	20
	Scene 4	21
	Scene 5	22
	Reviewing Act One.	24
	Act Two	28
	Start here	28
	Scene 1	28
	Scene 2	29
	Scene 3	31
	Scene 4	33
	Scene 5	35
	Scene 6	36
	Reviewing Act Two.	38
	Act Three.	41
	Start here	41
	Scene 1	41
	Scene 2	44
	Scene 3	46
	Scene 4	48
	Scene 5	50
	Reviewing Act Three	56
	Act Four.	60
	Start here	60
	Scene 1	61
	Scene 2	63
	Scene 3	65
	Scene 4	68
	Scene 5	68
	Reviewing Act Four	71

Act Five 77
Start here 77
Scene 1 77
Scene 2 78
Scene 3 79
Reviewing Act Five 82

Reviewing the Play 85

Con-Texts 91
A Radio Discussion of Romeo and Juliet 91
A Review of Baz Luhrmann's Film Version of
Romeo and Juliet 92
Screenplay of Romeo and Juliet 94

Teil III –
Klausurbeispiele

Petruchio's First Encounter With Katherina 98

Filmrezension: Zeffirelli's Romeo and Juliet 103

Discover ...: Zielsetzung und methodischer Ansatz

Die Shakespeare-Reihe *Discover ...* richtet sich an Schülerinnen und Schüler der Sekundarstufe II. Die Verfahrensweise lehnt sich an neuere lernpsychologische Erkenntnisse an. Das besondere Merkmal liegt in der Bearbeitung der Texte anhand von *pre-reading-*, *while-reading-* und *post-reading*-Aufgaben.

Pre-reading-Aufgaben führen zum Text, Thema oder Problem hin. Forschungsergebnisse belegen, dass eine interessante Texteröffnung einen positiven Einfluss auf die Textbegegnung hat. Die *pre-reading*-Aufgaben konkretisieren zudem besonders das Vorwissen und bauen Erwartungshaltungen auf. Spezifische *pre-reading*-Aufgaben finden sich in Form von Bild/Text-Collagen auf der in einen Akt einführenden „Start here"-Seite.

Beim ersten fortlaufenden Lesen kommen unterschiedliche textverarbeitende Operationen ins Spiel. Da hierzu in der Regel nur begrenzte Zeit zur Verfügung steht, ist eine Hilfstätigkeit darin zu sehen, beim Lesen von Zeit zu Zeit innezuhalten um auf das bereits Gelesene zurückzublicken. Durch das verlangsamte Lesetempo können intensivere Interaktionen zwischen Leser und Text stattfinden. Reflexions- und Verstehenshilfen finden sich in *Discover ...* in den *while-reading*-Aufgaben und Beobachtungsanleitungen in der Randspalte. Sie begleiten den Lesevorgang und dienen gleichsam als *navigational aid*. Mit ihrer Hilfe wird das Verständnis der Oberflächenstruktur des Textes sichergestellt. Diese methodische Neuheit wird durch ein besonderes Lay-out, durch die Unterteilung der Seite in eine Textspalte und eine die *while-reading*-Aufgaben enthaltene Randspalte, ermöglicht. Die mit Pfeilen versehenen Aufgaben begleiten den Lesevorgang. Sie haben vorwärtsweisenden, rückverweisenden oder statarischen Charakter. Ein nach unten weisender Pfeil (∀) verknüpft die Aufgabe mit dem nachfolgenden Text als so genannte Beobachtungsanleitung. Eine mit einem nach innen gerichteten Pfeil (◀) versehene Aufgabe bezieht sich auf die betreffende Textstelle und ein nach oben weisender Pfeil (∧) zeigt an, dass sich die Aufgabe auf den gerade gelesenen Textteil bezieht und man sich rückblickend Klarheit über das Textverständnis verschaffen soll.

Alternativ zum *guided reading* können die Aufgaben der Randspalte auch erst nach dem Lesen mündlich oder schriftlich beantwortet werden; ihnen kommt dann die Funktion der üblichen *comprehension questions* zur Überprüfung des Textverständnisses zu. In diesem Fall überlesen die Schüler während des ersten Durchgangs die Fragen und Aufgaben zunächst.

Die sich an die Szenen anschließenden *Activities* sind vertiefender Natur. Sie beziehen sich auf die kreative Textproduktion sowie auf die Interpretation im weitesten Sinn. Damit wird auch der textanalytische Zugriff geschult.

Die Kombination von *pre-reading-*, *while-reading-* und *after-reading-assignments (activities)* ermöglicht eine an neuesten lernpsychologischen und methodischen Erkenntnissen orientierte Textbearbeitung im Sinne einer vermittelnden Methode, bei der Lesende und Text gleichermaßen den ihnen zukommenden Stellenwert erhalten.

Klaus Hinz

Teil I

Discover ...
William Shakespeare:
Romeo and Juliet
Die didaktische Konzeption

Die didaktische Konzeption

Bedeutung der Tragödie *Romeo and Juliet* **für Jugendliche**

Für die heutige Jugend ist *Romeo and Juliet* nicht nur eine Tragödie, sondern auch eine Möglichkeit, die eigene Situation zu überdenken: "Because the play is a tragedy of youth as youth sees it, the young can bring to Romeo and Juliet an intuitive knowledge keener than they can bring, at this stage, to any other Shakespeare play. Identification with the two lovers can have a personal immediacy." (Veronica O'Brien, Teaching Shakespeare, London: Edward Arnold, 1982, S. 52).

Hierbei kann der Lehrer seine Schüler und Schülerinnen mit seinem pädagogischen Einfühlungsvermögen bei der Gewichtung der Analyseschwerpunkte sinnvoll unterstützen: "He must see to it that the play's most striking themes and effects have a chance to resonate as deeply within the student's being as possible." (Peter Roberts, Shakespeare and the Moral Curriculum, New York, Pripet Press, 1992, S. 37.)

Diese "striking themes" lassen sich wie folgt bündeln: Liebe versus Hass, Gewalt versus Zuneigung, Licht gegen Dunkel, christliches Denken im Vergleich zur Astrologie, jugendlicher Elan im Vergleich zur Lebenserfahrung der Alten.

Schließlich darf sich dieses Drama noch einer Reihe der schönsten Zitate aus der Feder des Barden und einer überbordenden Bildersprache rühmen, was bereits auf die großen Dramen der folgenden Jahre hindeutet.

Tabellarische Übersicht über die Szenen

Act	No. of scenes	Lines
1	5	707
2	6	620
3	5	783
4	5	396
5	3	426

Summary

Act, scene	Number of lines	Contents
1.1	232	Servants of Capulets and Montagues quarrel; Prince is angry; Romeo is madly in love with Rosaline, who has sworn chastity; Benvolio advises him to look at other beauties.
1.2	103	Paris asks Capulet for his daughter Juliet's hand in marriage; Capulet's servant meets Romeo in the street and asks him to read out the guests' names to him; Rosaline is one of the guests; Benvolio urges Romeo to go to Capulet's feast to make the acquaintance of other beauties.
1.3	106	The Nurse and Lady Capulet tell Juliet that the gallant Paris is keen on marrying her although she is even not 14 years old yet, a fact that does not bother Juliet's mother very much who gave birth to Juliet when she was even younger; Juliet answers that looking at Paris may perhaps lead to her liking him.
1.4	114	Romeo and Benvolio voice their different opinions as to going to Capulet's feast; Mercutio talks about idle dreams in his soliloquy concerning Queen Mab; Romeo, in the end, has a sudden premonition of an early death.
1.5	144	The exciting force: Romeo meets Juliet and is at once struck by her beauty; Tybalt hears his voice and, though reprimanded by his uncle, swears to revenge himself on Romeo for his intrusion on the feast.
2.1	42	Mercutio and Benvolio, still thinking that Romeo is in love with Rosaline, want to speak to him, but cannot find him.
2.2	189	The meeting of the two lovers: they have completely fallen for one another; their conversation ends in their mutual marriage vow.
2.3	95	Romeo tells his confessor, Friar Laurence, that his heart is set on Juliet, his enemy's daughter and asks him to perform the marriage rites.
2.4	192	Mercutio is backbiting Tybalt's qualities as a sword-fighter; the Nurse approaches Romeo with the news that Juliet is waiting for him; Romeo responds that he will wait for her at the Friar's cell to secretly marry her.
2.5	77	Juliet eagerly awaits the Nurse's return; when she is finally back she teases Juliet for quite a long time before she tells her to go to Friar Laurence's cell to be married to Romeo there.
2.6	37	The lovers meet in Friar Laurence's cell and, overjoyed, ask the Friar to begin the marriage rites which he performs at once.
3.1	193	The climax: Mercutio is slain by Tybalt by accident; in return Romeo revenges his friend and kills Tybalt; Benvolio urges Romeo to leave the market place before the Prince's arrival who may sentence him to death for disobeying his orders to keep the peace. Benvolio and Lady Capulet argue as to who is responsible for whose death. The Prince angrily responds to this turmoil by sending Romeo into exile.
3.2	143	This is an all female scene: Juliet sits longing to be with Romeo, when the Nurse enters the room and conveys the news to her that Tybalt is dead, killed by Romeo who in turn is banished from Verona; Juliet's anticipation of eternal bliss is shattered.

Act, scene	Number of lines	Contents
3.3	175	"Romeo is so deranged by the Prince's verdict which forces him to leave Verona that he threatens to kill himself in the Friar's cell. Banishment and a life without Juliet means death to him. The Nurse arrives at Friar Laurence's cell to inform Romeo that Juliet is waiting for him in her chamber to spend a last night with him before he has to leave for Mantua."
3.4	35	We are informed that Capulet has made up his mind to arrange Juliet's marriage to Paris for Thursday, i.e. in three day's time.
3.5	243	This is – apart from II, 2 – a highlight of the play. Juliet spends the night with her husband before he has to leave Verona. – The second part of the scene is about the confrontation between Capulet and his daughter Juliet who is unwilling to marry Paris. He threatens to banish her from household if she does not obey his will.
4.1	126	Juliet, in desperation, goes to Friar Laurence, asking him for help. She meets Paris there, who tells her that he is looking forward to Thursday. The Friar supplies Juliet, who threatens to kill herself, with a liquid that fakes death so that she can avoid marrying Paris.
4.2	46	The list of the guests being invited to the wedding is talked about when Juliet returns from confession and tells her father that she is sorry for her disobedience.
4.3	58	Juliet trusts the Friar and swallows the potion that will cause her "untimely death".
4.4	28	A seemingly unimportant scene: Capulet supervises the preparations for Juliet's marriage although it is very early in the morning; he is elated at the thought that he has arranged such a good match.
4.5	137	Juliet is found motionless on her bed, seemingly dead. The family is shocked but Friar Laurence assures them that Juliet is in a better place, i.e. in heaven. The musicians invited to play at Juliet's wedding behave in a rather irreverent way by making jokes about their job in complete disregard of the situation.
5.1	86	Romeo in Mantua is mistakenly informed by his servant that Juliet is dead and has been carried to the Capulets' tomb. He is so desperate that he buys poison from an apothecary and hurries back to Verona to join Juliet in death.
5.2	30	Friar Laurence's letters to Romeo which are meant to inform him of his actions have not been delivered because his fellow-franciscans were not allowed to leave Verona for fear that they had been infected by the plague, an event with fatal consequences.
5.3	310	Paris who wants to mourn Juliet's death sees Romeo at her tomb and thinks Romeo wants to desecrate the tomb. They fight and Paris is fatally wounded. Romeo covers his "dead" wife with kisses and drinks the poison. When Juliet awakes she finds the vial and, hearing the voices of the approaching wardens, stabs herself. Mourning their children's deaths the Capulets and Lord Montague whose wife has died of grief because of Romeo's banishment swear to end their family feud. The Prince, nevertheless, is furious at the outcome and promises to punish all who are guilty of this fatal ending.

Weiterführende Literatur

1. Bloom, Harold. *Shakespeare – The Invention of the Human,* London: Fourth Estate, 1999.
2. Donaldson, Peter S. *Shakespearean Films / Shakespearean Directors,* Winchester; Mass. and London: Unwin Hyman, 1990.
3. Fairservice, Don. *Film Editing – History, Theory and Practice,* Manchester: Manchester University Press, 2001.
4. Garfield, Leon. *Shakespeare Stories,* London: Victor Gollancz, 1985.
5. Gibson, Rex. *Teaching Shakespeare,* Cambridge: CUP, 1998.
6. Hayward, Susan. *Cinema Studies – The Key Concepts,* London: Routledge, 2000.
7. Jackson, Russell, ed. *Shakespeare on Film,* Cambridge: CUP, 2000.
8. Jackson, Russell and Robert Smallwood, eds. *Players of Shakespeare 2,* Cambridge: CUP, 1989.
9. Jeffcoate, Robert. *Starting English Teaching,* London: Routledge, 1992.
10. Kermode, Frank. *Shakespeare's Language,* London: Alan Lane, 2000.
11. Mckernan, Luke and Olwen Terris, eds. *Walking Shadows, Shakespeare in the National Film and Television Archive,* London: British Film Institute, 1994.
12. Ramm, Hans-Christoph. Juliet's Courage. Genderproblematik in Shakespeares, Zeffirellis und Luhrmanns *Romeo and Juliet* in einem LK Englisch 13/1, *Neusprachliche Mitteilungen,* Heft 4, 1999, 247–252.
13. Russin, Robert, U. and W.M. Downs, eds. *Screenplay: Writing the Picture,* Fort Worth: Harcourt College Publishers, 2000.
14. Timm, Norbert. „Shakespeare und seine Zeit. Vorschläge für prereading activities vor der Lektüre eines Dramas von Shakespeare", *Praxis,* Heft 3, 1996, 265–273.
15. Themenheft „Shakespeare medial", *Der fremdsprachliche Unterricht – Englisch,* Heft 46, Juli 2000.
16. Turner, Graeme, *Film As Social Practice,* London: Routledge, [3]1999.
17. Themenheft „Shakespeare kreativ", *Der fremdsprachliche Unterricht – Englisch,* Heft 56, März 2002.

Internet-Adressen

1. Globe Theatre London: www.shakespearesglobe.com
2. www.shakespeare.org.uk
3. Bremen: www.shakespeare-company.com
4. www.cummingsstudyguides.net → Shakespeare Study Guide
5. www.imdb.com → William Shakespeare

Filmography

1. *Romeo and Juliet, 1936,* Director: George Cukor, Norma Shearer (Juliet), Leslie Howard (Romeo), Music: Herbert Stothart.
2. *Romeo and Juliet, 1954,* Director: Renato Castellani, Juliet (Susan Shentall), Romeo (Laurence Harvey), Music: Roman Vlad. Prologue spoken by John Gielgud.
3. *Westside Story, 1961,* Directors: Robert Wise / Jerome Robbins, Maria (Natalie Wood), Tony (Richard Beymer), Music: Leonard Bernstein.
4. *Romeo and Juliet, 1968,* Director: Franco Zeffirelli, Juliet (Olivia Hussey), Romeo (Leonard Whiting), Music: Nino Rota.
5. *Romeo and Juliet, 1978,* BBC TV Shakespeare, Director: Alvin Rakoff, Juliet (Rebecca Saire), Romeo (Patrick Ryecart), Music: James Tyler.
6. *Romeo and Juliet, 1996,* Director: Baz Luhrmann, Juliet (Claire Danes), Romeo (Leonardo DiCaprio) Music: Nellee Hooper.
7. *Shakespeare in Love, 1998,* Director: John Madden, Screenplay: Marc Norman and Tom Stoppard, Actors: Joseph Fiennes, Gwyneth Paltrow, Judi Dench, Music: Stephen Warbeck.

Teil II

Discover ...
William Shakespeare:
Romeo and Juliet
Das Schülerbuch im Unterricht

Das Schülerbuch im Unterricht

Allgemeine Bemerkungen zum methodischen Vorgehen

Da es sich bei *Romeo and Juliet* um das Genre Drama handelt, sollten handlungs- und produktorientierte Aktivitäten im Vordergrund stehen. Nicht nur Überlegungen der Schüler und Schülerinnen über die Umsetzung der shakespearschen Zeilen in Handlung sind ein Desiderat, sondern auch die kritische Auseinandersetzung mit den angegebenen Filmen. An dieser Stelle sei empfehlend darauf hingewiesen, dass sich eine methodische Arbeitserleichterung für die Interpretation von *Romeo and Juliet* durch die Analyse des Films *West Side Story* in der Jahrgangsstufe 11 anbietet. Hier könnte nämlich das notwendige Fachvokabular bereitgestellt werden.

Um den Kursteilnehmern möglichst zeitig das Gefühl zu geben, dass es sich bei *Romeo and Juliet* nicht primär um einen Lesetext handelt, sondern um eine Vorlage für eine Theateraufführung bzw. um eine Umformung in ein *Screenplay,* sollen sie schon im Abschnitt „Getting started" zu handlungsorientierten Aktivitäten angehalten werden, wobei die Gruppendiskussion im Vordergrund steht.

Da Shakespeares Sprache – gut 400 Jahre nach seinen Theatererfolgen – nicht immer auf Anhieb zu verstehen ist, führt dies z. T. zu sehr intensiven Annotationen, die aber für die Diskussionen im Unterricht absolut notwendig sind. Hilfestellung leisten dabei die knappen Zusammenfassungen am Anfang jeder Szene.

In den am Ende jeder Szene aufgelisteten „Activities" sollen die Kursteilnehmer nicht nur auf das Verständnis der Szene überprüft werden, sondern in der Regel produktorientiert mit dem erworbenen Wissen arbeiten und ihre methodischen Fertigkeiten aus vorhergegangenen Halbjahren anwenden. Hier wird immer wieder auf die Beschäftigung mit dem Medium Film verwiesen, sodass die Schüler und Schülerinnen nicht nur Rezipienten sind, sondern auch kreative „Macher".

Die Textsammlung unter der Rubrik „Con-Texts" soll die Kursteilnehmer zusätzlich mit Meinungen und Standpunkten vertraut machen und sie nach Beendigung der Lektüre zur persönlichen Stellungnahme ermuntern, da die Zusammenhänge nun hinreichend bekannt sind.

Anmerkungen zum Prolog

Der Prolog hat zwei wichtige Funktionen mit Blick auf das elisabethanische Theater zu erfüllen: Einerseits werden die Zuschauer über den Schauplatz – *fair Verona* – informiert, zum anderen wird darauf hingewiesen, dass es sich um zwei aristokratische Häuser handelt, deren Einfluss im Stadtstaat Verona so groß ist, dass die ganze Stadt darunter leidet, wie es durch den Prinzen nach dem Gezänk auf dem Marktplatz in eindringlichen Worten geschildert wird. All dies macht dem heutigen *Leser* also keine Probleme. Da aber Shakespeares Drama damals nur auf der Bühne zur Kenntnis genommen wurde, waren diese Preliminarien durchaus nötig.

Enter Chorus*

Two households both alike in dignity*,
In fair Verona where we lay our scene,
From ancient grudge* break to new mutiny*,
Where civil blood* makes civil hands unclean.
5 From forth the fatal loins* of these two foes*
A pair of star-crossed* lovers take their life*;
Whose misadventured* piteous overthrows*
Doth with their death bury their parents' strife*
The fearful passage* of their death-marked* love,
10 And the continuance of their parents' rage,
Which, but* their children's end, nought* could remove*,
Is now the two hours' traffic* of our stage;
The which if you with patient ears attend*,
What here shall miss*, our toil* shall strive to mend.

                                                                       Exit

Annotations ▶

Chorus: in Elizabethan drama a character who speaks the prologue and other linking parts of the play
both ... dignity: the one as noble as the other
grudge: long-term hatred; **mutiny:** disorder, violence
civil blood: the blood of other citizens of Verona
from ... loins: as offsprings; **foes:** enemies
star-crossed: ill-fated, unlucky; **take their life:** are born
misadventured: unfortunate; **overthrows:** tragic accidents
strife: conflict; **fearful passage:** terrible course
death-marked: doomed to death; **but:** apart from; **nought:** nothing
remove: bring to an end; traffic: activity, performance; **attend:** listen to
what ... miss: that which I have left out in this prologue; **toil:** acting

Assignments ▶

1. In which modern media is this kind of condensed information used?
2. Sum up in two sentences what themes the play will deal with in the acts to come.
3. Would you see any advantages or disadvantages if this prologue were omitted ? Discuss.
4. How would you stage the Prologue in your own film or TV production?

◄ Solutions

1. This information in sonnet-form is frequently used at the beginning of the news, especially on BBC, Radio 4, thus giving the reader / listener the "headlines" of what is going to happen.
2. We are told that there are two families in Verona who hate each other because of a long-lasting feud. This causes severe problems to the children of the two houses because they have fallen in love with each other, a situation that is so threatening that Shakespeare calls them "star-crossed lovers".
3. This question is likely to start a general discussion in the classroom if a prologue like this is necessary or not.
4. It will be the teacher's task to either show the students the beginning of a film version as a help to their own activities or he may ask them to write a shooting script on their own if they are especially keen on doing so.

Act One

Start here

Love – hate – power ▶ p. 6

1. Try to define what the words 'love' and 'hate' mean to you and what role they play in people's lives.

   To start with, the definition of the words 'love' and 'hate' can be taken from a dictionary. Then we can try to define what feelings are experienced when people use these words.
   As an example: we can refer to the political development in the Balkans where people suddenly started hating each other because of allegedly religious or sometimes political reasons. Under these circumstances love between two people of different ethnic backgrounds hardly stood a chance of being accepted.

2. Find examples of love-hate relationships in literature. Show how the main characters were able or unable to cope with their situation.

   One of Shakespeare's plays that deals with a love-hate relationship is Othello. Iago's hatred for his master and general leads to Othello's and his own downfall and to Desdemona's unjustified death at the hands of her husband. See also Walter Scott, Ivanhoe, William Faulkner, The Sound and the Fury and soap operas such as The Denver Clan.

3. A famous German literary critic wrote in his *Memoirs* that "love is a blessing and a curse, a favour and a disaster". (Marcel Reich-Ranicki in *Mein Leben*). Would you agree with him? Discuss.

   The discussion may be highly subjective because the pupils may think of their own first experiences or might cite examples they know from literature.

Act 1 Scene 1

Assignments

While-reading tasks

p. 10 ▶ What is quite clearly Tybalt's plan?

While Benvolio has every intention of preventing the participants from fighting Tybalt is keen on quarrelling because he hates everybody associated with the Montague family.

Why does Lady Capulet call for a crutch? ◀ p. 10

Lady Capulet is, according to her own words (p. 21, l. 73), not more than 28 years old whereas her husband is much older (p. 28, ll. 30–32). She reminds him of his age and that he should not be taking part in a street fight.

Why is the Prince so angry? ◀ p. 11

It is the third time that these two old families have caused riots in the streets of Verona although it should be their first and utmost duty to keep the peace. He threatens to punish the abusers of the peace with death if they repeat their offence.

What does Benvolio try to prevent? ◀ p. 11

In his own words he emphasizes that he wanted to keep the men from quarrelling, but did not succeed, because in his opinion Tybalt was eager to fight the Montagues.

Why would Shakespeare use this word play in this context? ◀ p. 12

If the word 'sycamore' is used here ambiguously then Shakespeare makes Benvolio Romeo's mouthpiece because he knows that Romeo is on the verge of losing his sweetheart, i.e. he is sick at heart.

How does Montague describe his son's present state of mind? ◀ p. 12

According to his father Romeo lives under a cloud of misery. He shuns other people instead of enjoying life. Montague is troubled because he does not know why his son is so downhearted.

What does Romeo try to tell Benvolio here? ◀ p. 13

Benvolio mentions the word 'sadness' and has hit the nail on the head. Romeo is brooding over his bad luck, i.e. his unrequited love for Rosaline. Had he been in a happy mood the hours would have passed in no time, but at the moment it is exactly the other way round.

How does Romeo describe the situation in Verona? ◀ p. 13

By using a number of oxymorons Romeo points out the dissension in town. People seem to love killing each other unstead of working for peace. Romeo's unhappiness is mirrored in the citizen's zest for political and social chaos.

What kind of woman is Rosaline in Romeo's words? ◀ p. 14

Romeo complains about Rosaline's indifference towards him. He compares her to the goddes Diana who was the protector of women. He believes that her beauty will not survive posterity if she remains unmarried.
This passage can also be interpreted as follows: Romeo is aware of his manly qualities and is hurt in his self-esteem by Rosaline's rejection.

Activities

Setting the tone ▸ p. 15

1. If you were responsible for designing the scenery what would you do to make this enmity between the two families visible to the audience?

Every teacher should be reminded of the fact that a play is meant to be performed. Thus a group of students of about 18 years will be motivated to discuss the setting of the first scene. Teachers might know the film versions of this play. So it will have to be decided what the group would like to achieve: writing a film script or a script for a performance in the school hall. One question remains to be answered: will it be a very modern setting or rather a 16th century or even a medieval setting? The pupils will certainly have some ideas of their own.

2. Why do you think minor characters are the first ones to appear on the stage?

From a dramatic point of view Shakespeare knew that the audience's attention first had to be attracted at the beginning of the play. This can be done in many ways. Here Shakespeare makes the two servants of the Capulet household, Gregory and Sampson, talk about the problem in a rather obscene way, which the 'lower' classes in his time would definitely have enjoyed. Apart from giving the audience the information necessary in order to understand what the whole play is about, they also set the tone as to what is going to happen in the next two or three hours on the stage. They talk about the ongoing situation, whereas the major characters act and/or react in a special situation; very often they are talked about – at least at the beginning of the play.

The power of words ▸ p. 15

1. Why does Shakespeare change from prose to verse in line 58?

There are two reasons. Firstly, Benvolio, a major figure, enters the stage and calls for the parties to stop fighting. His language is not colloquial or slangy like the expressions of the servants. Secondly, Tybalt, another major figure, is introduced and the audience senses very quickly that he is the "bad guy" who will dominate the scene for a while. So Shakespeare's language sets the tone: it is no longer playful or informal, it is now used to designate the changing mood of the scene.

2. What linguistic device does Romeo use in lines 169–176 ?

When we listen to or read these lines we may simply call them paradoxical. These utterances – e.g. loving hate – combine two terms which in everyday language are complete opposites; this rhetorical antithesis emphasizes very sharply what Romeo thinks of the situation going on in Verona.

Hero or lame duck? ▸ p. 15

1. What is it that makes Romeo look so melancholy?

We know that Benvolio makes Romeo utter the words "Out of her favour where I am in love" (l. 162). In other words, although her name has not yet been mentioned, we know that Rosaline has given Romeo the brush-off. As a result, Romeo feels lovesick. Later we learn that

Romeo's state of mind can quickly change – from a joyful to a pensive or even sullen mood.

2. What do lines 222–231 tell us, the audience, about his state of mind?

Romeo is unable to forget his love for Rosaline. He compares the days without her with a man having lost his eyesight. But when he asks Benvolio to show him a lady that is more beautiful than Rosaline there is anticipation in the audience: His wish will very soon come true because in the evening he will meet Juliet at her father's feast. You are Romeo's friend and would like to help him overcome his problem.

Write a letter to an 'Agony Aunt' in which you ask her to advise you how to help Romeo forget Rosaline.
Letter writing is often a very good task for students to freely voice their opinions and to offer solutions to typical problems at their age.

◄ **Asking an agony aunt for advice p. 16**

Look again at lines 179–188. Do you think Romeo's words are: pathetic / ridiculous / bombastic / superb? Or does he resent Benvolio's questions? What do these lines describe?

Romeo's words are without doubt pathetic and bombastic because he behaves *like* a callow young man who can only perpetuate stereotypes and cliches he has picked up somewhere. He does not resent Benvolio's questions because he is a genuine friend he can always trust. All in all, these lines show us a still immature young man who has not learned what it means to fall in love or to lose a friend. His feelings of love would better be called puppy love.

Act 1 Scene 2

Assignments

While-reading task

What do these lines tell you about the servant?

◄ **p. 17**

The servant's mental abilities are definitely poor because he muddles up everything. He is plainly ignorant of what kind of tools the shoemaker or the tailor need for their jobs. Being illiterate he looks for someone to read out the names of the guests to him as written on the list.

Activities

1. What do you think Lord Capulet was discussing with Paris before entering the stage? Write a short introductory dialogue (work in pairs).

◄ **Guessing a topic p. 19**

Capulet: Well, well what a terrible quarrel this was. I should like to know what made the servants start this row. I think we are now going to be held responsible for their action, if you know what I mean.

Paris: As a matter of fact, I saw some of the Montague servants attack your men from behind. That was not very fair, if you ask me. I think I will have a word with uncle Escalus in order to calm him down. I really wonder why he was so angry with *you* …

2. What dramatic effect is created by Capulet talking to Paris about marrying his daughter?

The fact that the name of the play is *Romeo and Juliet* makes us anticipate that danger is imminent; Shakespeare increases the tension as early as in the second scene. The audience knows that this can easily lead to a clash between Paris and Romeo. As we know, this really does happen but not until the end of the play.

What's in a name? ▶ p. 19

Look up the word 'benevolence' in your dictionary. Use your findings in order to explain why Benvolio is the appropriate person to give Romeo some good advice.

The word *benevolence* comes from the Latin words 'bene volens' and means "well wishing". Benvolio is not only Romeo's cousin but also a close friend whose aim it is to keep the peace in Verona, and who wants to help his friend in this rather tricky situation after Rosaline has made it clear that she is not interested in Romeo.

Act 1 Scene 3

Assignments

While-reading tasks

p. 21 ▶ What is your first impression of Juliet's Nurse?

The Nurse is to Juliet what Mercutio is to Romeo, a very close friend. It was the Nurse who suckled Juliet when she was a baby because her own child Susan had died in infancy; that is why she loves Juliet with all her heart (cf. 61–63). But she is wordy and highly ambiguous when she thinks back on her married life with her late husband. The best example can be found in lines 43–45. She is good-humoured because she takes life as it is; she is such a windbag that even Lady Capulet has problems in stopping her flood of words.

p. 22 ▶ Has the Nurse really understood what Lady Capulet is talking about?

Whereas Lady Capulet tries to describe Paris's qualities to Juliet the Nurse interferes by making one of her rather bawdy remarks (l. 96);

this is typical of her earthy sense of humour. The Nurse is not interested in a man's good character.

Activities

1. How do they try to persuade Juliet to get married soon?

> Friendly persuasion? p. 23

Lady Capulet does not know how to begin the conversation, but the Nurse's outcry "And I might live to see thee married once" is the cue for her to ask Juliet what she thinks of getting married. Juliet is taken aback but listens to her mother's arguments. First she mentions that "ladies of esteem are made mothers" although they are younger than Juliet. Then she describes Paris as a very good-looking man, a fact that the Nurse especially emphasizes. We can conclude that the Capulets, though aristocrats, would definitely improve their social position in Verona because Paris is the Prince's relative.

2. Characterize Juliet's nurse. Make a list of her positive as well as her negative qualities.

positive	negative
seemingly caring	wordy and vulgar
good-humoured	bawdy, even a bit obscene
loyal to the Capulets	superficial

Write Juliet's entry in her diary as to what she thinks about getting married in the near future. Work in pairs.

> A binding contract – so soon? p. 23

Some clues:
What does it mean to fall in love? / have no friend to ask for advice / still too young / mother had already given birth when she was younger than I am now / have I got a duty to obey my parents in this matter? / looking at men cannot do any harm, can it?

Act 1 Scene 4

Assignments

Additional while-reading task

Why is Romeo unwilling to dance (ll. 11–12)? Do you think his excuses are appropriate?

> p. 23

Romeo is still sick at heart because he realises he will never win the heart of Rosaline. He knows from the servant's list that Rosaline is invited to Lord Capulet's party. His friends' excitement is understandable but he feels downhearted at the moment as he cannot be merry in her presence.

Activities

Intruding upon a private celebration p. 26

There is a party under way in your city or town which you want to go to at all costs. Work out – in pairs or small groups – a plan that will ensure you can attend this party. Then listen to the results and decide what plan/trick would be the best to achieve your aim.

It is difficult to decide what your students' reaction to this question may be. They very often have clever, sometimes even crazy ideas as to what to do in such a situation. Let them work. If you think it not worth dealing with such a task leave it out.

Amusing eccentricity? p. 26

1. To what extent does this tale differ from the normal fairy tale?

A fairy tale, in general, is a story about "mysterious pranks and adventures of supernatural spirits who manifested themselves in the form of diminuitive human beings. These spirits possessed certain qualities such as supernatural wisdom and foresight and the power to regulate the affairs of man for good or evil." (C. Hugh Holman, ed. A Handbook of Literature, New York: The Odyssey Press, 1972, p. 218).

Mercutio talks about Queen Mab, "the fairies' midwife". The origin of the name is uncertain but may come from the Celtic 'Mabh', a Welsh word meaning 'child'. Mabh was believed to be the chief of the Irish fairies. Being a 'midwife' means delivering sleeping men of their fancies, i.e. "the children of an idle brain" (l. 97) as Mercutio says. Whatever qualities Mercutio gives Queen Mab, it can be stated that his speech is a foreboding of things to happen – to him as well as to Romeo.

2. How do Romeo's premonitions of his premature death fit into this rather informal and lively atmosphere?

Going to a feast celebrated by his greatest enemy is without doubt a real danger. Romeo is furious when he sees the wounded people being taken to hospital. This exaggerated fear he shows is part of his present melancholic mood.

In this context it should be mentioned that Franco Zeffirelli in his film emphasizes Romeo's critical situation by a bell chiming at exactly the moment when Romeo talks about his "untimely death" (l. 111). Cf. Hemingway's For Whom the Bell Tolls.

Act 1 Scene 5

Assignments

While-reading tasks

p. 30

"Well said, my hearts!" – Who is Capulet speaking to?

Tybalt is furious about Romeo attending this feast. He wants to throw him out, but his uncle, Capulet, strictly forbids him to do so.
Standing among his guests Capulet has two things to do: on the one hand he has to calm down Tybalt, on the other hand, with a forced smile on his face, he makes casual and complimentary remarks to his guests passing by.

What do you think they whisper in Capulet's ear?

◀ p. 31

It is rather certain that the maskers are about to leave Capulet's house and as a matter of fact whisper an excuse in his ear, telling him why they are no longer able to take part in the merriments although light refreshments are being served.

Activities

1. Does love at first sight still happen today?

◀ Stuck on her – at once!
p. 33

There will be students who may start a long discussion on this topic whereas others may not like to talk about it. So let the students decide how to handle this delicate matter.

2. What is, nevertheless, the first hint that their love is doomed?

Romeo has just seen Juliet and not yet spoken a word to her while Tybalt is quarrelling with his uncle about Romeo's "intrusion". Romeo is unaware of the impending danger. This moment when Tybalt leaves the stage (l. 92) and Romeo begins his love affair with Juliet is the **exciting force** as it begins the conflict of opposing interests.

Capulet's party is a feast people in Verona will have heard about. Write a report for the society column of a newspaper about this party. Do not forget that the vocabulary you use is dependent on what newspaper you write for.

◀ Socializing with some friends
p. 33

When the students have decided what newspaper (serious / popular press) they want to write this report for, excerpts of the two film versions (Zeffirelli = serious press / Baz Luhrmann = popular press) will help them a great deal in performing the task.

Look again at lines 93 – 106. What poetic form has Shakespeare used to express the feelings the lovers have for each other? Why?

◀ Poetry in motion
p. 33

At Shakespeare's time and even earlier the sonnet form had become one of the great favourites of the educated citizens in Europe. In this context, using the sonnet form means expressing one's feelings in a very emotional way. It is the poetic beginning of a passionate relationship.
The allusion to the word 'pilgrim' gives these lines a religious background. Romeo has not travelled a long way to a holy place for purely religious reasons, he has found his 'angel' just around the corner (cf. Baz Luhrmann's film), but on enemy territory – and that will cause problems soon.

Reviewing Act One

The playwright ▶ p. 34

William Shakespeare wrote comedies, e.g. *A Midsummer Night's Dream*, histories, e.g. *Henry V* and tragedies such as *Hamlet* or *King Lear*.

1. Which group does *Romeo and Juliet* belong to?

If the students do not know the end of the play they may conclude so far that it is a history because there are two influential families and a Prince in Verona. The families' quarrels may end in civil war but this is only a supposition. Our utmost interest, of course, will be to find out what will happen to the two lovers in the acts to come.

2. After having dealt with Act One do you think it's worth reading this play?

This will be an open discussion in which the students can voice their opinions.

3. Are the problems mentioned so far relevant to you today?

A friendship breaks up, parents ask their child to think about getting married, "civil brawls" have on three occasions caused troubles in Verona's streets. The fact that a friendship comes to an end is human and understandable. The question remains how we ourselves solve such a problem. There has been no change throughout the centuries. It is still common today in parts of the world that girls are married to men they do not know nor love. Civil wars have not only caused havoc in Europe, cf. the Balkans, but especially in other parts of the world, cf. Afghanistan. So there is a lot to talk about.

The characters ▶ p. 34

Draw a genealogical table of the two families.

The Capulets	The Montagues
Lord and Lady Capulet	Lord and Lady Montague
Juliet, their daughter	Romeo, their son
Tybalt, cousin to Capulet	Benvolio, Montague's nephew

1. Collect as many details about the main characters of the two houses either from what they say about themselves or from what others say about them.

Benvolio who appears first on the stage can easily be characterized by what he says. He is a man who wants "to keep the peace" (I.1 62). In contrast to him Tybalt is fiery and hostile to every member of the Montague family: " I hate hell, all Montagues, and thee" (l. 65). Capulet and Montague though both have passed their middle-age join the fight without knowing what the causes for the row are. Lady Capulet even ridicules her husband by calling for a crutch. This highly ironical remark may already reflect a strained relationship between a rather young mother (hardly older than 26 years) and a much older husband (Zeffirelli's film has made a wonderful scene of it, cf. p. 17, ll. 12–13). A visual means in order to save a lot of words… Romeo is sick at heart – not only because he has just been given the brush-off, but also because he hates these 'civil brawls' in Verona (p. 13, ll. 159–176). Juliet is surprised at her mother's request to think about marriage, but she obediently tells her that she will consider it: "I'll look to like, if looking liking move" (p. 22, l. 98) – what a wonderful means of using alliteration.

Lord and Lady Montague are shown seemingly interested in their son's well-being (p. 12, ll. 110–149) but do not talk to him face to face.

That has to be done by Benvolio.

First conclusion: Juliet lives in a family where father and mother are no longer shining examples of a happily married couple, whereas Romeo seems to be roaming the streets as he cannot / will not talk about his problems with his parents.

2. You are asked to stage this first act in school. Which of your friends in class, which of your teachers would you ask to take part in a performance of this play? Say why they are best suited for their roles.

This is a first attempt at a theatre performance. There will always be students as well as teachers interested in theatrical activities, for sure, but it may not be everybody's cup of tea.

Choose short passages from the text you think characterize the following persons best:

◀ **The language p. 34**

Romeo can be described best when we refer to the following lines: I,1 – 165–175 ; I,4 – 106–113, I,5 – 93–96. These passages characterize a youngster undergoing doubts, fear and heavenly bliss.

Mercutio: I,4 – 27–32; 53–95; 96–103 . This is Mercutio: lively, sometimes sarcastic, jesting; a clear contrast to melancholy Romeo. One question, nevertheless, may be asked: Why are we introduced to Romeo's friend Benvolio first before Mercutio enters the stage?

Benvolio: I,1 – 62–63; 112–124; I,2 – 45–50. He is not made for quarrelling; he is sensitive, good-hearted, a real nice guy, an adviser and someone who can listen to other people.

The Nurse: I,3 – 17–49; 76–77; 96. The Nurse is a chatterbox, sometimes unpleasantly direct in her speech and garrulous. She is the foil to innocent Juliet, she is a sex-ridden, coarse woman whose wordiness can sometimes be highly annoying.

Tybalt: I,1 – 60-61; I,5 – 55–59; 89–92. He is the troublemaker 'par excellence': in a western movie he would be the bad guy. He has triggered off the series of violent events so far.

What linguistic devices has Shakespeare used to give each character his / her own profile?

Romeo, at the beginning, is 'in love with love' as is the Duke in *Twelfth Night*. He resorts to cliches and expressions that have lost their freshness (cf. I,1 – 179–180; 184–187). But this way of expressing himself changes abruptly when he meets with Juliet. Suddenly he seems to outgrow these childish attitudes and seems to begin a new life.

Juliet is rather shy and reserved; in her 'conversation' with her mother she only speaks when she is asked and is careful not to hurt anybody's feelings. When she meets Romeo she carefully chooses her words before she finally yields to his charm and persuasion.

Mercutio is the foil to Romeo: very often witty, intelligent, shrewd, eloquent, down to earth. He is juicily gossipping when he talks about Romeo's relationship to Rosaline.

Tybalt's choice of words shows from the beginning that he is of an aggressive nature. Everything he says is meant to start a quarrel. Though his uncle can prevent him from doing harm to Romeo he threatens, when withdrawing from the scene, to revenge himself on Romeo.

The Nurse plainly shows that her educational background is poor. Whenever she speaks her words are very ambiguous and full of sexual allusions.

Benvolio is a youngster who chooses his words carefully and never gives cause for a fight. He is plain-spoken and trustworthy.

You will have obtained information about the Italian poet Petrarca by now.

1. What kind of poem was he the creator of?

Petrarch or Francesco Petrarca (1304 – 74) was born in Arezzo, Italy. He gave the sonnet his name. In 1341 he was crowned poet-laureate in Rome. The sonnet form he created can be divided into an octave and a sestet. The octave can be subdivided into two quatrains so that we can say that the sonnet consists of three parts rhyming abba / abba / cde /cde. The Petrarchan sonnet was introduced to England by Sir Thomas Wyatt (1503 – 42). Later, poets such as Milton and Wordsworth made use of it.

2. What is the difference between the lines the Chorus speaks (p. 33. ll. 144–157) and the poem using the Petrarchan pattern? (As a help compare the lines the Chorus speaks with William Wordsworth's poem "Composed Upon Westminster Bridge").

The Petrarchan sonnet and the English or Shakespearean sonnet differ in their rhyme schemes. The Shakespearean sonnet can be subdivided into three quatrains and a concluding couplet, in other words the rhyme scheme runs like this: abab / cdcd / efef / gg, whereas Wordsworth's poem rhymes as follows: abba / abba / cdc / dcd. As we see, Wordsworth has introduced a variant to Petrarch's sestet.

Masquerade ▶
p. 34

1. Why is wearing a mask necessary for Romeo and his friends?

The host of the celebrations is Capulet, the Montagues' "greatest enemy". So it is absolutely necessary for Romeo and his friends to wear a mask, otherwise they would not have been allowed to take part in the feast. In spite of these precautionary measures Tybalt overhears Romeo speaking to someone and is so furious that a Montague has been allowed to enter that he starts quarrelling with his uncle about Romeo's presence.

Unknown maskers normally danced for a short time at the feast, then paid compliments to the host before leaving the house (cf. I,5 – 121–122).

2. In spite of Romeo wearing a mask at Capulet's feast he is not able to mask his feelings for Juliet. How does this endanger his own life and Juliet's life?

According to Capulet Romeo is "a portly gentleman" (p. 29, l. 66) and "Verona brags of him" (l. 67); in other words Romeo would not have had any problems with the 'Master of the Celebrations'. But there is always a fly in the ointment and that is Tybalt's hatred towards the Montagues. As he hates hell and 'all Montagues' (p. 10) he will definitely find a way to 'eliminate' Romeo, not only because he is a Montague, but also because he has intruded into Capulet territory, something that the quarrelsome Tybalt cannot stand.

The fact that Romeo meets and falls in love with Juliet endangers not only his own but also her life because Juliet is Tybalt's cousin. He would do everything to undermine their friendship and especially to prevent their marriage.

Act Two

Start here

Surmounting difficulties? p. 35

"He ran this way and leapt this orchard wall". – Have a close look at the picture. Imagine you are in Romeo's place. What may the balcony – so high – stand for?

This photo shows the "original" balcony in Verona and, as we can see, it will be rather difficult to climb it in order to reach Juliet's room. This balcony – so high – is a sign of the seemingly insurmountable obstacles that separate the two families.

Act 2 Scene 1

Assignments

While-reading tasks

p. 36

Where do you think Romeo would hide on the Elizabethan stage?

The stage, at Shakespeare's time, did not have a curtain, so when Romeo wants to hide from his friends it can only be done by hiding behind one of the large pillars or behind one of the doors (see picture).

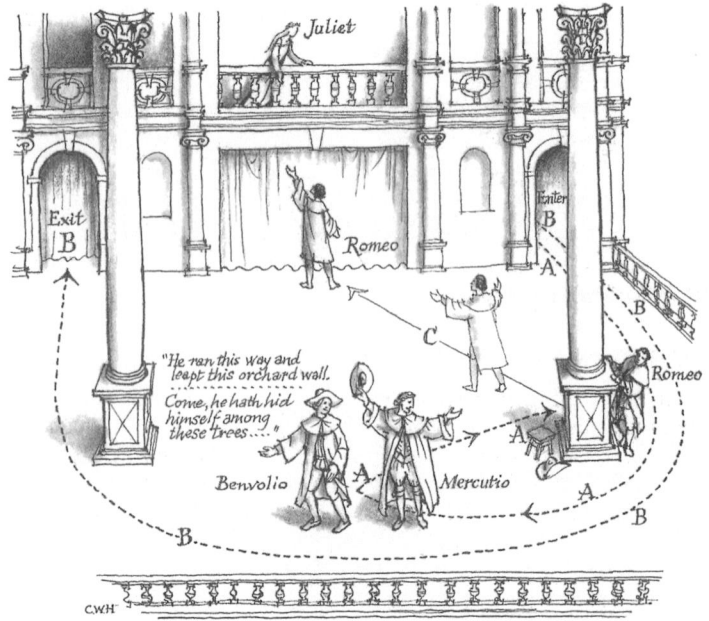

How does Mercutio describe Rosaline here? ◀ p. 36

Mercutio still thinks that Romeo is in love with Rosaline and thus vividly describes her advantages: her 'high forehead', l. 18 – an Elizabethan symbol of beauty – and the 'quivering thigh', l. 19, an allusion to sexual intercourse. He speaks of Romeo as if he is dead; so his ghost must reappear in the figure of Romeo.

Activities

Mercutio's speech is full of ambiguities and sexual allusions.
1. Why does Mercutio behave that way? ◀ Womanizer or jester? p. 37

With reference to Act 1, Scene 4 we have learned that Mercutio has problems with the true values of love and so Shakespeare uses him as a foil to Romeo who only has eyes for Juliet.

2. Compare him with Benvolio.

Both are Romeo's friends but their characters are completely different. Benvolio is the honest, down-to-earth companion who helps Romeo wherever he can whereas Mercutio is lively, intelligent but also afraid of losing his friend to a woman. Women are nothing more than "bunnies" to him a man can play with; a sign that he is incapable of falling deeply in love. The sentence "thou a poperin pear", l. 38 can be an allusion to a hidden homoerotic tendency in Mercutio.

3. Which of them would you call Romeo's "better friend"?

This task will give the students ample opportunity to put forward their arguments as to who may be Romeo's best friend, but it will be a very personal view, indeed.

Act 2 Scene 2

Assignments

While-reading tasks

Why does Romeo compare Juliet with the sun? ◀ p. 38

When morning breaks the sun rises in the east and this is what Romeo is talking about: It is the beginning of their profound love and when he sees her standing on the balcony she is the source of light to him. Juliet is the sun and their love will be constant, no longer to be disputed. The sun here is seen in oppositon to the 'inconstant moon', l. 109.

"tis not to me she speaks": Who does Romeo address now? ◀ p. 39

p. 39 ▶ Imagine the Elizabethan apron stage. Romeo is surrounded by the spectators and it is them that he speaks to.

Can you understand why lots of people say this is one of the most famous scenes in world drama?

Comparing a woman's eyes to the stars was nothing special but Shakespeare elaborates here on Juliet's beauty in a way that is not only new but illuminating; especially revealing is the physically intimate image in lines 24–25 which tells us that Romeo is not only deeply in love with Juliet but that he explicitly longs for her in a very sexual way.

p. 39 ▶ "What's Montague?" What does Juliet try to express here?

After hearing the news that Romeo is a Montague – Act 1, Scene 5, 136–137 which shocked her, Juliet now looks at the matter from a practical point of view. She is in love with Romeo so much that even his name can no longer prevent her from dedicating her life to him.

p. 40 ▶ What image does Romeo use in lines 82–84?

Romeo compares himself to a navigator who, in search of a precious pearl, will travel around the world in order to find it even if this means meeting his death. So from the beginning of their love affair death is lurking around the corner.

p. 41 ▶ What does Juliet mean in lines 131–132?

This is Juliet's second meeting with Romeo and as she is convinced that she loves him dearly she gives expression to her feelings, hoping that their love may bloom and prosper and should still be steadfast when they meet next time, i.e. next morning.

Activities

Good-bye, my love, Rosaline! p. 44 ▶ Compare Romeo's speeches in Act 1, Scene 1 – 202–218 and 222–231 – with Act 2, Scene 2 – 1–23.
1. How has Romeo's attitude towards love changed now that he has met Juliet?

In Act 1 Romeo is terribly disappointed by Rosaline's stubbornness to reject his amorous advances. He is angry that she wants to dedicate her life to chastity, i.e. to the services of the goddess Diana. Her refusal undermines his self-confidence a great deal. Apart from that, he is convinced that her beauty outshines that of all other girls. Juliet, on the other hand, has returned his love at once. According to the Elizabethans' belief, lovers could only fall in love at first sight, if it was true love at all. And Romeo has completely fallen for Juliet. He wants to be so close to her that he wishes to be her 'glove' in order to touch her cheeks as often as possible. Although he desires to make love to Juliet he restrains himself. He is no longer the superficial young boy; he has learned his lessons in love.

2. Can we, on the other hand, assume that Juliet's love for Romeo is sincere? Find passages in the text to support your answer.

Very early in the text we know that Juliet's love for Romeo is sincere; especially lines 33–36 tell us that she will even give up her name if this could lead to a happy ending. Later – lines 116–124 – give us absolute certainty that Juliet has made up her mind to plan a life with Romeo without further ado.

Why was the sentence spoken by Romeo "But soft! What light through yonder window breaks?" not only the romantic outcry of a love-sick boy at Shakespeare's time?

◄ **Imagining day and night**
p. 44

Plays at Shakespeare's time began at two o'clock in the afternoon, in other words the spectators very often had to imagine what was going on on the stage according to the plot. As there were hardly any stage directions at this time sentences like this one gave clues as to what was happening on the stage at this particular moment or where something was going on.

If you were the director of a film version of this play how often would you use a close-up in this scene and to what purpose?

◄ **Access to a person's mind**
p. 44

One of the sentences that definitely urges a director to use a close-up is Romeo's question "O wilt thou leave me so unsatisfied?" (l. 125). Here it is Juliet's facial reaction we are interested in as this question in itself has a highly sexual undertone. Other examples would be the last lines of Romeo's monologue (23–25) – or his last words of this scene (ll. 186–189). Lines 139–141 refer to Romeo's sentence in Act 1, Scene 4, l. 49 where he said that he "dream'd a dream tonight". It was night then and Romeo thought of "some consequence yet hanging in the stars" (l. 107); Now it would be interesting to see his mimics while he is speaking these words: "I am afeard / Being in night, all this is but a dream / Too flattering-sweet to be substantial" (ll.139–141).

A film director should always be reminded of Goneril's words in King Lear where she tells her father "I love you more than word can wield the matter" (i.e. than words can convey – Act 1, Scene 1, l.56). It is his task to ask his cameraman to convey visual images to the audience as this is one of the advantages of film-making.

Act 2 Scene 3

Assignments

While-reading tasks

What is the friar talking about?

◄ p. 44

Friar Laurence has special knowledge about the properties of the plants that populate his garden. Poisonous plants may turn out to be life-saving if used correctly (e.g. ll. 15–19). Look especially at these opposing expressions "grace and rude will" (l. 28) meaning nothing else but 'good' and 'evil'.

p. 45 ▶ What does Romeo refer to here?

The audience know what Romeo is talking about; the word 'rest' is closely related to the word 'relaxation' here, i.e. "an enjoyable activity which helps you to rest and stop thinking about something" (Longman Language Activator, 1993, p. 1125). It is quite clear to the audience/reader that Romeo's meeting with Juliet was a highly enjoyable event – something the friar is not yet informed about.

p. 46 ▶ What does this line tell us about their relationship?

Friar Laurence and Romeo have a close relationship, the friar is Romeo's spiritual guide. Their relationship can be compared to that between Juliet and her nurse. As we can read Friar Laurence is well informed about Romeo's attempts at making contact with Rosaline (ll. 77–78).

p. 46 ▶ How can the Friar's tone be described here?

'Doting' means being "foolishly or excessively fond of somebody" (COD, 1996, p. 405). So Friar Laurence's tone may be called sympathetic but mixed with a critical undertone. In other words he knows that Romeo is still an adolescent with all his ups and downs, who has to learn his lessons of life.

p. 47 ▶ What effect does the use of alliteration create in this line?

Alliteration is a rhetorical device which is often used in poetry as well as in prose for the sake of emphasis or for creating a musical effect. Romeo is in harmony with Juliet and, according to the Elizabethans, harmonious music was always used to establish a dramatic mood or to intensify an emotion.

Activities

Establishing contact with the audience p. 47 ▶ 1. Why is Friar Laurence introduced to the audience by means of a soliloquy?

To begin with, a soliloquy in a Shakespearean play is meant to inform the audience of what is going on in a character's mind (cf. Hamlet's 'To be or not to be'); furthermore, it often gives information about the action that has already happened or may soon begin (cf. the beginning of R III). In this play we learn quite a lot about Friar Laurence's activities and his way of life. He is rather good-natured and knows precisely what can be done with the herbs he is just collecting. All this may help the audience to understand that he is able to mix the sleeping potion he later-on offers Juliet when she is completely downhearted (cf. Act 4, scene 1).

2. Romeo is able to overhear part of the friar's speech. Is there a link between the friar's words about the healing power and destruction of certain herbs and Romeo's speech at the end of Act 1, Scene 4 (106–113)?

Romeo's utterance of "veil forfeit of untimely death" (l. 111) may be remembered here. The poisonous herbs the friar speaks of will be the tripping device for Romeo's death when he buys poison from an apothecary in Mantua.

How would you react to a person who tells you that he/she stands "on sudden haste" in getting married?

◀ **Love or lust?**
p. 47

We may be surprised or even amazed at Romeo's desire to get married so soon after being jilted by Rosaline; it seems that he will no longer wait for the bliss of marriage and its consummation. It is surely this sexual craving that makes Romeo act so quickly. Friar Laurence warns him ("wisely and slow", l. 95) but agrees to help him because he thinks this is the chance for ending the enmity between the two families.

Act 2 Scene 4

Assignments

Time: Monday noon

While-reading tasks

Why is Mercutio afraid of Romeo meeting Tybalt?

◀ p. 48

Mercutio may have overheard Tybalt's words at Capulet's feast. Apart from that, he still believes that Romeo is in love with Rosaline and in this mood Romeo is not Tybalt's equal should it come to a fight, especially as Tybalt is known to be a very experienced sword-fighter.

Why does Mercutio still talk of Rosaline?

◀ p. 49

Benvolio and Mercutio have no idea about what happened during the night when Romeo ran away from them. Mercutio is convinced that Romeo spent the night with Rosaline making love to her; at least this is his interpretation of Romeo's words "business was great" (l. 45).

What is it that makes Mercutio Romeo's dearest friend?

◀ p. 49

Mercutio is Romeo's best friend because he is an extrovert and lively person. His sanguine temperament is a contrast to Romeo's reserved behaviour. He is the planner whose enthusiasm can win people over to his side. His negative characteristic is his rashness which finally causes his death. Whenever he is together with Romeo he talks of love but means nothing else but sex. Maybe this is the reason why Romeo hesitates to tell him of the last night's big encounter with Juliet.

p. 50 ▶ Why does Mercutio use such obscene language?

Mercutio seems to have never had a girlfriend. He is a kind of 'gang-leader' who feels at home when he is together with his male friends with their bawdy, sometimes even crude language.

p. 50 ▶ What is the Nurse's use of malapropism a sign of?

The Nurse is infamous for her wordiness. She has belonged to the Capulets' household for such a long time that she thinks she can talk about everything and will always find the right word for it. Her education is rather low which is best shown here when she mixes up the words 'confidence' and 'conference'.

p. 51 ▶ How does Benvolio react to the Nurse's misuse of words?

Benvolio, though not a very witty boy, reacts quickly and ridicules the Nurse by using the word 'indite' (put a speech into words / write a letter) instead of using the word 'invite'. If she had used the right expression "I desire some conference with you" she would have expressed herself in a highly formal way which does not befit her way of talking.

p. 53 ▶ Why does Romeo change from prose to verse?

Romeo has 'forgotten' his two friends he has just made jokes with. It is now his young wife he is thinking and talking of and the use of verse is a wonderful way of showing his strong and deep affection for Juliet.

Activities

To cut or not to cut?
p. 54 ▶
1. If you had been asked to direct this play would you have decided to cut this scene
   – completely
   – to a certain extent
   – not at all?
   Why, why not?

This will be an open discussion in which the students will put forward their arguments. It may be interesting to listen to their reasons for or against cutting the scene.

2. We are given more information about Mercutio in this scene.
   a) How would you describe his character now?
   b) Has your attitude towards him changed in reference to Act 1?

Mercutio is without doubt the 'star' of this scene. On the one hand, he mocks Tybalt because of his way of fencing, on the other hand, he makes fun of all people subjecting themselves to the contemporary fashionable ways of speaking. He seems to be the most energetic and vivid person so far who hardly has any problems to solve. Benvolio is left the role of a bystander.

The question if our attitude towards him has changed in reference to Act 1 is not easy to answer. It will be very interesting to hear the students' pros and cons in this discussion.

If we think of the time this play was first acted on the stage what could have been reasons for the long passages in prose?

◀ **Prose versus verse** p. 54

When we talk about the Elizabethan theatre we know that it was highly popular among all levels of society. In other words, the theatres were full of aristocrats as well as ordinary people and in order to remain popular it was the playwright's task to serve all social classes by using all levels of language – from the very formal to the colloquial or sometimes even vulgar.

How does the Nurse behave in this scene? Is she very eager to please Juliet as an intermediary between her and Romeo?

◀ **A helping hand?** p. 54

The Nurse behaves rather ambiguously; on the one hand, she seems to support Paris in his 'battle' for Juliet (ll. 178–183); on the other hand, she warns Romeo not to harm Juliet by making indecent advances (ll. 145–147). All the same, we gain the impression that she is quite happy to help Juliet in the preparations for the wedding (l. 154).

Act 2 Scene 5

> **Assignments**

While-reading tasks

Why does the Nurse pretend to be so tired?

◀ p. 55

At this moment the Nurse knows more than Juliet and she takes delight in teasing her by pretending to be tired in order to hold back the news for a while. In Shakespeare's theatre this was a good example of comic relief especially for the lower classes.

Why does the Nurse suddenly fall back into speaking prose?

◀ p. 55

These two women have been living together for the last twelve years and have developed a very close friendship. But they do not belong to the same social class which is made clear here. Juliet's language is rather graceful at this moment whereas the Nurse is absolutely plainspoken in her comments on Romeo.

Is the Nurse's behaviour silly or just amusing?

◀ p. 56

This is one example of Shakespeare's mastery at achieving a highly dramatic effect from simple material. Juliet wants the Nurse to break the news to her about when Romeo is going to marry her but the

Nurse's response to Juliet's curiosity seems to be complete indifference. Her abrupt question "where is your mother"? (l. 56) must have had a hilarious effect on the Elizabethan audiences. All in all, the situation may look silly but from a theatrical point-of-view it is highly amusing.

Activities

> **A caring relationship p. 56**

This scene concentrates on the relationship between Juliet and the Nurse.
1. Describe Juliet's emotional state of mind at the beginning and at the end of this scene.

This short soliloquy (ll. 1–17) reflects Juliet's impatient mood. She has been waiting for three hours now. In her youthful impatience she mocks her Nurse's lameness (l. 4) and would prefer her to "be as swift in motion as a ball" (l. 13). The Nurse's arrival turns out to be emotionally stressful to Juliet until the final sentence gives relief to her tortured soul: "Go; I'll to dinner, hie you to the cell" (of Friar Laurence / l. 76). At this moment Juliet is convinced of having reached the pinnacle of her dreams: In a little while she will be Romeo's wife. Now her impatience has turned into pure delight.

2. Why do you think the Nurse makes such a fuss about being so tired before telling Juliet to go to church and meet her Romeo?

From a dramatic point-of-view her evasiveness is understandable and intended: The longer Juliet waits for the Nurse's answer the more the dramatic tension increases. So Shakespeare succeeds in making a mountain out of a molehill.

3. Is the Nurse's saying (l. 75) a sign of a certain lasciviousness or just a rude joke?

The Nurse's language is sex-ridden and an example of her vulgarity. Although she complains about Mercutio's behaviour (Scene 4, ll. 132–143) her words are as open to ambiguity as Mercutio's.

4. What is the dramatic function of this scene?

This scene is the theatrical prelude to what will happen in Friar Laurence's cell. With eager anticipation Juliet waits for the moment of 'eternal bliss'.

Act 2 Scene 6

Assignments

While-reading tasks

> **p. 57**

Is the Friar's 'sermon' a sign of his uneasiness or happiness in helping to arrange this marriage?

Romeo urges the Friar to begin the marriage ceremony as quickly as possible so that Friar Laurence is afraid of Romeo's haste. In his short 'sermon' he tells Romeo that passion may be exciting but is very often short-lived. He warns him not to act too quickly because he who is too fast will arrive as late as those who are rather slow. So the Friar's task is to cool down Romeo's high spirits of youth.

Describe Romeo's mood at this moment. ◀ p. 57

Romeo is overjoyed because as he has just said, being united with Juliet for "one short minute" (l. 5) means entering heaven to him. He only waits for her to say 'yes' (ll. 26–29) and he will even defy death (l. 7).

Activities

There is a saying that clandestine marriage acts do not lead to a happy end.
1. What is your opinion in this matter?

◀ Marriage without parental consent p. 58

This is an open discussion; the teacher may refer to Shakespeare's tragedy *Othello* in which Desdemona secretly marries the Moor, which provokes a strong confrontation between her and her father who feels deceived by her as well as by Othello.

2. How do you judge Friar Laurence's attitude towards love now in comparison to his earlier views (II, 3)?

We know that the Friar often rebuked Romeo about his silly advances towards Rosaline because he said it was merely foolish love (Act 2, ll. 81–82) and he thought that Romeo's attempt at showing his love to Rosaline was nothing else but 'bookish' (l. 89).
Now the situation has changed: he sees that these youngsters only have eyes for each other; this is why he willingly agrees to unite them in holy matrimony, although he certainly knows that this secret marriage may turn out to be problematic.
Shakespeare idealizes marriage in this scene. Romeo, however, does not seem to be able to get rid of his scruples because even at this moment of utmost joy he talks about death: "Do but close our hands with holy words / Then love-devouring death do what he dare" (ll. 6–7).

Shakespeare leaves out the actual marriage ceremony. Write this scene.

◀ Creativity! p. 58

Before the students start writing they should be informed that Shakespeare deliberately left this scene out. The Friar is a representative of Catholicism and in the 1590s it might have caused riots to present such a scene on the Elizabethan stage; anything popish was strongly resented by the people.

Reviewing Act Two

Playing with words
p. 58

Mercutio's way of speaking is characterized by his use of puns.
1. Find examples in this act.

Punning was an Elizabethan pastime; it was part of the dramatic art of a playwright, and Shakespeare was a master of this art.
Mercutio is the wittiest character in this play and takes every occasion to use puns. We find quite a lot of puns in Act 2, Scene 4 where Mercutio is at his best.
Let's mention only a few examples: In line 44 there is the word 'slip'; It can mean a) slip away and b) a counterfeit coin. A bit later (ll. 46–47) we find the word 'case'; it can mean a) situation and b) physical condition. Mercutio alludes to Romeo's nightly 'activity', i.e. making love to Rosaline. Another pun is used in l. 99. The word 'prick' suggests different meanings: a) point and b) penis. A last example can be seen in Mercutio's song (ll. 117–122). The word 'hoars' can mean a) turns mouldy and b) goes whoring. In other words, a sexual undertone can be found in all the examples mentioned above.

2. Where do they come from?

These puns are almost completely taken from the sexual word-field. On the one hand, Mercutio's relish for using these words is a sign of his intelligence, on the other hand they display his verbal rudeness.

3. Why does he use them?

Playing with words, working with the ambiguities of words was a fascination Shakespeare was very much attracted to. As far as Mercutio's rudeness is concerned we may take his surroundings into consideration. His way of expressing himself may be explained psychologically. Though Mercutio belongs to the upper classes he is confronted with the same problem as a lot of rich youngsters of today: He lives a life of idle self-satisfaction, very often close to self-destruction because he is a rich young man who utterly lacks emotional warmth.

Text into performance
p. 58

Look at lines 33 – 69 of the second scene.

1. In pairs, prepare this passage for a stage performance.
2. Read the lines clearly and aloud, keeping to the metrical structure of the verse.
3. Find out where there is a sudden change of tone.
4. Now add mimics and gestures to your way of speaking so that they help to express your intentions.
5. What would be the ideal setting for this scene if you were to make a modern film version of this scene?

This is a dramatic approach to a selected passage of Act 2, Scene 2. This assignment will give the students the chance of working with a text passage with the intention of preparing a film version or a theatre performance. It will help them to look at this passage anew and from a theatrical point-of-view. Although this is seldom done in the classroom it may lead to a much better understanding of the play as a whole.

Have a closer look at the beginning of the third scene.
1. What is the function of a soliloquy?

> ◀ **Analysing a soliloquy** p. 59

A soliloquy, especially in the Elizabethan theatre, was a speech spoken by a character alone on the stage; he either was thinking aloud for the benefit of the audience or he was willing to communicate his plans to the listeners (cf. Iago in Othello or Richard III – the beginning of the play).

2. What do we learn about Friar Laurence from this soliloquy?

First of all, he knows a lot about the herbaceous plants in his garden. Apart from that, he is characterized as a pleasant and likeable person. Finally, he is important for the promotion of the plot.

3. Do you think that a soliloquy is an appropriate element of the theatre conventions in the 21st century?

G.B. Tennyson writes in his book "An Introduction to Drama": "Most of these (i.e. Elizabethan) conventions of dramatic language are not found in the modern theater because they tend to weaken the illusion of reality ..., the loss of the soliloquy may well be the most regrettable, because this convention enabled the playwright to penetrate character as deeply as any novelist or poet." (New York: Holt, Rinehart and Winston, 1967, p. 36) This quotation can be the start of a highly interesting debate among the students.

The Nurse often makes the audience smile because of her rather drastic way of expressing herself. The Elizabethans called this theatrical element comic relief.

> ◀ **Comic relief** p. 59

1. Why was comic relief especially used in tragedies?

In a tragedy comic relief was often used to provide relief from emotional intensity, and, by contrast, to heighten the seriousness of the story. According to this defintion we see that Shakespeare has introduced Mercutio and the Nurse to enrich and deepen the tragic implications of the action.

2. Find more examples of comic relief in the second act.

The Chorus after speaking its lines at the end of Act 1 has just left the scene when Benvolio and Mercutio begin calling Romeo's name. Mercutio makes fun of Romeo's attraction to Rosaline although the audience know that she is out of the 'race' – a very good example of dramatic irony. All this serves to introduce the great scene that is to follow in Juliet's garden. Amusing, as well, is the passage in Scene 4 when the Nurse enters the stage in order to speak to Romeo; it is the interplay between her and Mercutio that makes people laugh (ll. 109–124).

Exercising media literacy p. 59	Choose any passage of Act II which you think is important to your understanding of the play and write a film script of it. Work in pairs or small groups.

In this activity the students can follow the example of Craig Pearce and Baz Luhrmann (cf. pp. 133–139).

Act Three

Start here

"Come night, come Romeo. – Hang thee, young baggage! Disobedient wretch!" – What do you think Juliet's problems will be?

◀ **The burden of love** p. 60

When we look at these two pictures we may find the following answers:
On the one hand, Juliet yearns for her lover to spend the night with her.
These are not lustful thoughts because she is now Romeo's legitimate wife. – But, as the second picture indicates, something seems to have gone wrong. The sentence 'disobedient wretch' can only have been spoken by her father who must have asked Juliet to do something she is not willing to accept or agree to.

Act 3 Scene 1

Assignments

Time: Monday afternoon

While-reading tasks

What is Mercutio angry about?

◀ p. 61

Mercutio is in a mercurial mood: he wants to fight and Benvolio tries everything to talk him out of it. Mercutio cannot understand that an Italian like Benvolio is resentful of a good fight and so he is very angry with him.

Why does Mercutio call his sword a fiddlestick here?

◀ p. 62

Mercutio intentionally misunderstands Tybalt's "thou consort'st with Romeo" (l. 41); Tybalt means 'you keep company with him', whereas Mercutio answers Tybalt as if he had said 'you play music with Romeo'; music, however, was played by minstrels, in other words by servants. That, of course, is an insult in Mercutio's eyes and a reason for him to start a fight. Thus his sword becomes his fiddlestick or baton, and he is keen on being the 'conductor' of this fight.

Why is Romeo eager to stop Tybalt fighting against Mercutio?

◀ p. 63

It is not only Romeo's intention to stop the fight because "the Prince expressly hath forbidden bandying" (ll. 83–84) but also because of the fact that he has become Tybalt's cousin after marrying Juliet.

| p. 65 | **What are the two meanings of 'grave'?** |

Although fatally wounded Mercutio cannot stop using a play on words; 'grave' can mean a) serious, sober, i.e. not in the mood for making jokes and b) a burying place, tomb. So even in the face of death he cannot stop making funny remarks.

| p. 66 | **Why does Tybalt come back after leaving the market place?** |

It is hardly understandable that Tybalt comes back after having killed Mercutio; the only explanation may be that he cannot forget that Romeo went – uninvited – to the Capulets' feast and that his fury is still so unbridled that he wants to vent his anger on Romeo. We should not forget that he had called Romeo 'a villain' (l. 57) only a couple of minutes ago.
And the news that Romeo in the meantime has become his cousin has not been conveyed to him.

| p. 66 | **What does Romeo want to express?** |

Now it is Romeo's turn to be furious. His reputation has been stained (l. 107) and his best friend, Mercutio, is dead. This fight will decide who is the next to follow him (to his grave).

| p. 67 | **Is Lady Capulet full of grief or simply prejudiced?** |

Tybalt is the son of Lady Capulet's brother; so the relationship between them is rather close. It is difficult for us to decide what Shakespeare's intention was; when we have a look at the two films (Zeffirelli and Buz Luhrmann), we see that Tybalt is Lady Capulet's 'favourite' to put it mildly. According to the interpretation of these two films we can definitely say that she is full of grief at having lost her 'beloved' Tybalt. As we know from the text that Lady Capulet was twelve years of age when she gave birth to Juliet, Tybalt and Lady Capulet will have been almost of the same age.

| p. 67 | **What does Lady Capulet accuse Benvolio of?** |

Lady Capulet, in her grief, is not willing to believe what Benvolio says. She accuses him of being Romeo's accomplice and that makes him a liar in her eyes.

Activities

| Rebellious subjects! p. 68 | Verona is in turmoil. Again, the Prince's subjects have disobeyed his order for peace. |

1. You are a special correspondent for either 'The Sun' or 'The Guardian' Write an article about this incident that has lead to two deaths.

Here is an example as it may have been published in 'The Sun':

Romeo Montague Must March to Mantua
Mercutio and Tybalt dead and Romeo exiled

Details are hazy, but it appears that young Romeo was trying to pacify the situation when it all went wrong.

"Originally Tybalt appeared and tried to pick a fight with Romeo," said Benvolio, who saw the whole thing. "When he refused to fight, Tybalt fought with Mercutio instead. Romeo tried to get in between them and stop it. But as he held him, Tybalt stabbed Mercutio."

Although Tybalt ran off, he returned later. By this time Romeo was ready to revenge his friend's death.

"Tybalt came back and Romeo fought him and killed him. I think he felt responsible for Mercutio's death", said Benvolio.

Exiled

The Prince decided that Romeo should be exiled from Verona.

"He's devastated", said Benvolio. He keeps on about his wife, but I know for a fact he isn't married. I don't know where he's gone tonight, but the state he's in I don't know what he'll do."

Wherever Romeo has gone, he will have to leave Verona tomorrow morning or die.

"It's not the end of the world," said his father. "He'll probably enjoy it in Mantua. Maybe he'll find a nice girl and settle down."

Text (not headline) taken from: Nick Page, The Tabloid Shakespeare, London: HarperCollinsPublishers, 1999, p. 141.

2. Montague and his wife have just heard of the events in the market place. Write down what they are talking about and what conclusion they come to.

Lady Montague: "I told you, but you wouldn't listen. Look at our son. Instead of leaving for Bologna to start his studies there he's fighting this bloody Tybalt. If he isn't fighting he spends his time with this nymphet Rosaline or writes love poems on walls and trees. Have you ever seen such nonsense? What will ever become of him? I wonder …"

Lord Montague: "Come wife, let's be fair. What did he do? He revenged his best friend's death. I always said this Tybalt was a rat-catcher. So why bother about his death? We can be lucky: Romeo is sent to Mantua by the Prince. Great. That isn't too far away. He will learn his lessons of life there. Don't forget: he's still a bachelor …"

3. Form three groups in your class: one supporting the Capulets, the second the Montagues, the third the Prince's household. Discuss how to solve the situation without blaming either familiy.

In this activity it may be worth having a 'hardliner' and a 'compromiser' in each group in order to lead an animated, sometimes even heated discussion about this controversial topic.

4. Does a close friendship as the one between Romeo and Mercutio justify an emotional reaction like this?

From today's point-of-view this reaction is hardly understandable, at least not in a European country. But in the early 15th century other rules had to be taken into account. First of all, Tybalt calling Romeo a villain was an insult that only an 'effeminate' (l. 110) man would have endured. Second, his reputation would have been at stake if he had not reacted to Tybalt's offensive behaviour. To any bystander Romeo's inactivity would have looked like cowardice. His hesitation to fight can only be explained as a result of his marriage to Juliet and his reluctance to be involved in a 'battle' between cousins.

Act 3 Scene 2

Assignments

Time: Monday evening

While-reading tasks

p. 70 ▶ How would you describe Juliet's state of mind (ll. 1–31)?

This scene is, from a dramatic point of view, a highlight on any stage. Juliet's anticipation of a wonderful night with her loving husband is suddenly smashed by the news the Nurse brings to her. It is a very good example of dramatic (tragic) irony because the spectators already know that Juliet's hopes of a wonderful future have completely been shattered by Fortune's terrible wheel.

p. 70 ▶ Why does the Nurse keep Juliet in the dark about what has happened?

The Nurse's words may, in terms of modern psychology, be described as sadism. Intentionally or unintentionally, she inflicts pain on the poor soul.
As listeners or members of an audience we may draw the conclusion that she wants to show us which family she sides with and it is definitely not that of the Montagues. It is a first hint that she forsakes her allegiance to Juliet and Romeo (cf. p. 87, ll. 218–220).

p. 71 ▶ Can you explain Juliet's violent outburst?

Juliet's reaction, at first sight, is understandable because the Nurse's words, up to this moment, are an excellent example of mind-manipulation. She describes Tybalt as "the best friend I had" (l. 61) and an "honest gentleman" (l. 62) so that it is quite clear to every listener / viewer what her opinion of Romeo is. Juliet, on the other hand, is highly irritated because she has only been Romeo's wife for only hours (l. 99).

p. 71 ▶ How do you judge the Nurse's statements about Romeo and men in general?

The Nurse quickly agrees to Juliet's harsh criticism of Romeo by stressing that all men are deceivers. When we take into account what the Nurse has said so far about the other sex we immediately recognize that she only trims her sails to the wind.

Who does Juliet speak to?

◀ p. 71

Only informed by the Nurse about what has happened in the market place Juliet begins a kind of inner dialogue with her husband. After having rebuked him for Tybalt's death she quickly recovers from her shock and comes to the conclusion that her tears are foolish (l. 102), because it would have been a catastrophe to her if Tybalt had killed her husband.
What causes her to grieve is the fact that Romeo is banished and, therefore, cannot make plans for their future togetherness.

Why has the Nurse not told Juliet much earlier about Romeo's whereabouts?

◀ p. 72

The situation is a bit tricky: the Nurse was not in the market place when Romeo killed Tybalt and was urged by Benvolio to leave the place at once. So we can only guess that she heard from somebody that Romeo was hiding in Friar Laurence's cell, in other words, her knowledge as to Romeo's whereabouts is Shakespeare's idea and finally helps to end the scene.

Activities

In Baz Luhrmann's film Juliet's soliloquy – shortened – is inserted between Tybalt killing Mercutio and Romeo killing Tybalt.
Do you think the director's decision is an advantage or disadvantage to the course of action?

◀ Film versus text
p. 72

Baz Luhrmann's film is no longer a mirror reflecting medieval Italian life; his characters are 20th century people who know that only he who draws his gun faster than his opponent will survive. Juliet's shortened monologue "Come, gentle night" set in her bedroom symbolises an oasis of calm surrounded by a sea of warring gangs. From this moment onward it is quite clear that the action will pick up speed until its fatal ending – from a cinematographer's point of view a highly effective means to attract audiences to his film.

Compare Juliet's language in lines 1–31 with Mercutio's in the first scene.

◀ Comparing people's language
p. 73

The first difference is that Juliet's soliloquy is written in verse, it is blank verse at its best. Mercutio very often speaks prose when he is on the stage. Moreover, Juliet talks about her intended consummation of her love in a dignified and pure way whereas Mercutio's language is that of a fighter, a desperado who does not give a damn about anything. That is why Mercutio's way of speaking is often aggressive or highly ironical whereas Juliet speaks with deep emotion about her longing for Romeo.

True allegiance? ▶
p. 73

The more we learn about the relationship between Juliet and the Nurse, the more we are irritated by the Nurse's behaviour.
1. Do you think the Nurse's grief is genuine or a hoax?

We know that the Nurse has been working for the Capulets for almost 14 years. In these years she has developed a close relationship to Juliet and to the family as a whole; she can even talk to Capulet in a way that a servant would better not do if he / she didn't want to be thrown out of the house (cf. Act 4 Scene 4, ll. 7–9). We can therefore come to the conclusion that her grief at Tybalt's death is genuine, especially as he was Lady Capulet's 'favourite' – a liaison she quite certainly knew about.

2. As soon as the Nurse leaves Juliet to find Romeo, Juliet sits down and writes an entry in her diary. What feelings and emotions might she confide in her diary? Write this entry.

Dear Diary,

What a disaster … My love, my Romeo – exiled!! How strongly had I wanted night to come to spend the hours with him, he that was my *day in night* … The Friar has sealed our love but we have not enjoyed it … What can I do? Burst into tears? No, never! I will wait for him until he is allowed to return to Verona. Where must he go? How long will he have to go?
I think I will have a word with the Prince … How shall I manage this? I must proceed very carefully in this matter. Lord, give me strength …

Act 3 Scene 3

Assignments

While-reading tasks

p. 73 ▶ What does the Friar try to convey in this conversation?

Friar Laurence is angry at Romeo's reaction. He tries to tell him that the Prince's decision to banish him must be accepted as it is only "body's banishment" (l. 11) instead of "body's death" (l. 11).

p. 74 ▶ Why does Friar Laurence react so angrily to Romeo's outburst?

Friar Laurence cannot understand Romeo's behaviour. He tries to explain to him that it was the Prince's goodwill that has kept him alive. So he should be grateful to the Prince instead of lamenting bitterly over his destiny.

p. 74 ▶ What is Romeo's state of mind at this moment?

Romeo's dream of a happy future with Juliet is completely shattered. He is convinced that a life without her is only another way of sentencing him to death. Banishment is more unbearable to him than death.

Act Three 47

What does Romeo accuse Friar Laurence of? ◀ p. 75

Romeo accuses the Friar of being insensitive to his problem because he cannot put himself in his place.

What kind of stage direction is given in this line? ◀ p. 75

Shakespeare was not only the playwright but a member of the actors' company as well. Today it is generally accepted that most of the stage directions in Elizabethan plays are the author's rather than the prompter's. But at Shakespeare's time it was often so loud in the theatre because of the audience eating and drinking and even shouting that an actor (here it is the Friar) had to bring it to the other actor's notice that someone else was about to enter the stage as it happens at this moment: "one knocks" (l. 71). This sentence is a warning to Romeo to hide as the Friar does not know who is going to enter the stage.

How does Juliet feel according to the Nurse? ◀ p. 76

The Nurse tells Romeo that Juliet cannot stop weeping about Tybalt's death – information that we have to view with caution – and continues calling Romeo's name. The Nurse's words already ring hollow here. She is no longer fully dedicated to the well-being of her protégée, Juliet.

Why is Romeo so dissatisfied with himself? ◀ p. 76

Romeo rebukes himself sharply for what he has done because he thinks that Juliet cannot forgive him for killing her relative.

What advice does the Friar give to Romeo in this long speech? ◀ p. 77

Friar Laurence is very angry with Romeo because of his lamenting and "unreasonable fury" (l. 111). He admonishes him for being ungrateful to himself and Juliet: "Thou pout'st upon thy fortune and thy love"(l. 144).
He advises him to stop crying and to go to Juliet's chamber in order to "comfort her" (l. 147). He promises him help in every way possible as long as he has to live in Mantua and to find ways to "beg pardon of the Prince" (l. 152). But he warns him to leave Verona before the guardsmen begin their duty at the gates because it will be his death if they get hold of him.

How does the Nurse react to the Friar's long speech? ◀ p. 77

The Nurse is completely awestruck by Friar Laurence's wisdom and well-founded arguments.

Activities

1. Romeo reacts very emotionally when he hears that he has been banished. Do you think that this verdict is a reason for him to try to commit suicide? ◀ Tired of life? p. 78

We should remember what it meant in the Middle Ages to be exiled by law from one's native town or city. Although Mantua is less than

40 kilometres away from Verona it is not the distance that upsets Romeo. It dawns on him after being married to Juliet for less than four hours that he will never be allowed to return to Verona without the Prince's consent. This idea frightens both of them. Banishment means nothing else than death to them. It also means that he has to abandon the city which has been the centre of his life and activities. So from an emotional point of view we may understand that he is weary of life; from a rational standpoint, however, we will come to the conclusion that he has not learned his lessons of life and reacts much more impulsively than Juliet.

To a certain extent, Romeo reacts so 'unreasonably' because of the Nurse's indifferent behaviour: Instead of telling him at once that Juliet is waiting for him in her chamber she mentions Juliet's reaction to Tybalt's death (but weeps and weeps, l. 99), thus adding fuel to his intention to commit suicide.

2. The Friar and the Nurse meet each other for the first time. What may have been Shakespeare's intention in doing so now?

Up to now the Nurse has been Juliet's confidante and the Friar Romeo's spiritual adviser. In the second scene of this act (l. 141) we have heard that the Nurse knows about Romeo's whereabouts – although Shakespeare does not tell us who has given her this information. It is the Nurse's task to urge Romeo to come to Juliet's chamber because he must leave for Mantua early in the morning without being seen by the guardsman.

Farewell to Benvolio p. 78

Why do you think Benvolio is no longer Romeo's companion and adviser after Mercutio's death?

After Mercutio's death and Romeo's secret marriage Shakespeare is concerned about the destiny that awaits these two lovers. It is only Romeo and Juliet now that have to reach decisions. From now on, the play concentrates on their efforts to come to terms with a hostile world. Benvolio, good-natured as he is, can no longer help Romeo cope with his problems.

Act 3 Scene 4

Assignments

While-reading tasks

p. 78 Why is old Capulet so sure about calling Paris his 'son'?

Shakespeare has already prepared us / the audience for what is happening now. In Act 1, Scene 2 we have learned that Paris has the intention of marrying Juliet (l. 6). Capulet is very pleased with Paris wooing his daughter but thinks that he should wait "two more summers" (l. 10). Now the situation has changed: after Tybalt's death he is glad that he can arrange Juliet's marriage to Paris because he is convinced that "she will be ruled in all respects by me" (ll. 13–14) without being consulted. Lady Capulet knows from her conversation with Juliet (Act 1, Scene 3) that she is quite willing to consider marrying Paris.

Why does Capulet ask these questions? ◀ p. 79

Lord Capulet feels rather guilty because of his sudden change of mind. He knows that such a decision causes problems as the time may be regarded as inconvenient – so shortly after Tybalt's death.

Who is Capulet talking to? ◀ p. 79

Having fixed the date for the marriage Capulet is now completely satisfied with the preparations under way and wants to retire to his bedroom. He asks a servant to show him to his room with a lamp in his hand.

Activities

Juliet's parents decide on her future on their own as was the custom at that time.

◀ Preparing Juliet's marriage p. 79

1. Capulet and his wife consider the pros and cons of Juliet getting married to Paris. Who dominates this parental conversation? Write a short sketch of it.

Capulet: Now it is up to me to do what your father did when I was wooing you, do you remember?

Lady C.: Of course, I remember; I was very young – twelve years of age – and very shy.

Capulet: Young you were, indeed, and rather shapely. Well, I didn't mind marrying you then, my lovely virgin … (aside) wouldn't know if I might repeat it today …

Lady C.: Tut, tut, don't make me blush; I knew that I had to obey my Father, especially as he was a paragon of virtue.

Capulet: (mistakenly) Ah, that's good to hear. Me – a paragon of virtue.

That is why I have made up my mind to get Juliet and Paris to church on Thursday. – Our daughter is young, not as young as you were then but Paris is the Prince's kinsman. Such a marriage can never be to our disadvantage. I think they will be a perfect match. I am sure you'd agree, wouldn't you?

Lady C.: Of course, my darling; have I ever given room for complaint?

Capulet: No, indeed, never; that's what I like best about you …

2. Write a short characterization of Paris.

TIME MAGAZINE
December 1, 2001

Paris – Verona's Bachelor of the Year

"He is a darling, handsome and modest, the perfect example of a gentleman". That is what Rosaline, 18, a distant relative of his, told us. Well, to tell the truth, she has hit the nail on the head.
A young man with a bright future to boast of. A relative to the Prince – the best ticket for a political career.
"What are your next plans?" we wanted to know when we had the chance of talking to him yesterday. "I can't tell you now but we are doing our best."
What a cryptic answer. But as we have heard from a reliable source Paris is about to get engaged and the lady in question is rumoured to be Lord Capulet's daughter, young and beautiful Juliet.
More in next week's edition.

Verona, 1 December

3. Do you find it acceptable that Juliet keeps her marriage a secret instead of telling her parents? Discuss.

Questions that may be brought up in this open discussion:

1. Are there compelling reasons for her not to speak to her parents about her relationship with Romeo?
2. Does she deceive her parents or doesn't she?
3. Has she developed in the course of time (Act 1, Scene 3 to Act 3, Scene 2)?
4. Does her strong affection for Romeo isolate her from those people she knows and cherishes?

Act 3 Scene 5

Assignments

While-reading tasks

p. 81 ▶ What does Shakespeare want to express with lines 9–10?

This is a striking example of Shakespeare's use of imagery: Night's candles, i.e. the stars, can no longer be seen because a new morning is about to dawn – "jocund day stands tiptoe on the misty mountain tops".

p. 81 ▶ Why does Juliet criticize the lark's singing?

Juliet is angry at the lark's singing because it is "out of tune" (l. 27), in other words the Lark's song is not harmonious to her ears. The explanation she offers is easy to understand: it is daybreak and time for Romeo to go, and she does not know for how long this will be.

What does Juliet seem to anticipate? ◀ p. 82

At this moment, Juliet is doubtful whether they will see each other again; Romeo's departure for Mantua is a journey into the unknown. For a girl of her age that has spent her life only within the walls of Verona 'parting is such sweet sorrow' (p. 43).

What did 'fortune' signify at Shakespeare's time? ◀ p. 82

The goddess Fortuna was known to most Elizabethans as the pilot of destiny. The other, more familiar image was 'the wheel of fortune' on which kings and princes rose to power but could not help falling as the wheel did not stop turning around. Juliet wants to express here that fortune's unreliability may turn out to be their advantage, i.e. she hopes that the Prince's order to banish Romeo may be reversed.

What do Juliet and Lady Capulet talk about? ◀ p. 83

They talk about different people. Whereas Lady Capulet believes that Juliet is in tears over her cousin's death, Juliet is sad about Romeo's banishment.

What part of the sentence does *dead* belong to? ◀ p. 83

The whole passage (ll. 93–95) is highly ambiguous in meaning: Juliet wants her mother to interpret her words as follows: 'I won't be satisfied until Romeo has died' whereas she means quite clearly that she will be Romeo's love until he dies. It is very difficult for Juliet to hide her feelings as Romeo has just left her bedroom after consummating their marriage.

What does Capulet compare Juliet's body to? ◀ p. 84

Her father sees her weeping and compares her to "a bark, a sea, a wind".
(l. 131). Her eyes stand for the sea with its low-tide and high-tide, her body resembles a ship that is sailing "in this salt flood" (l. 134), the wind reminds him of her sighs she is breathing for Tybalt – at least he thinks so.

Is Capulet justified to scold Juliet so severely? ◀ p. 85

Is it his disappointment over Juliet's decision not to marry Paris? Why does he suddenly hasten to get Juliet to church? In his first meeting with Paris he urged him to wait "two more summers", but now he seems to have changed his mind completely. Let's hear what Michael Bogdanov, a well-known director of the 'English Shakespeare Company' has to say about Capulet's behaviour: "It's nothing to do with Fate or the stars; it's greed and avarice on the part of Capulet insisting that his daughter marries someone close to the seat of power: Escalus's nephew Paris …
(It is) the desire of Capulet to cement his position in society." Graham Holderness, ed. *The Shakespeare Myth,* Manchester: MUP, 1988, pp. 94–95.
This quotation can be copied and given to the students to start a discussion, especially as they now have enough information about the Capulet family.

| p. 85 | What may be the Nurse's reason for defending Juliet so strongly? |

As we have heard before, the Nurse has been in the service of this household for about 14 years. Because of this long period of time she has established a relationship of personal trust with the family and therefore thinks herself entitled to interfere in this family dispute and to defend her dearly beloved Juliet.

| p. 86 | How do you think Juliet feels at this moment? |

Juliet feels extremely unhappy. She is dumb-founded when she hears her father's harsh reaction to her refusal to marry Paris within three days. The deep agony she experiences is even intensified by her mother's lack of support.

| p. 86 | Is Lady Capulet hard-hearted or only unkind to Juliet? |

It is clear from the beginning that Capulet is a domineering person in the family. Lady Capulet has certainly not learned in her fourteen years of marriage to influence her husband's decisions, she has quietly obeyed his orders. Therefore her reaction to Juliet's plea for help cannot be regarded as hard-hearted but rather as a sign of her utter failure as a mother.

| p. 87 | Why does the Nurse advise Juliet to forget Romeo? |

At this moment the Nurse reveals her moral weakness and her shallow way of thinking concerning interpersonal relations. At this very point her failure to respond to Juliet's problem ends the close friendship that had developed in the last fourteen years between these two women. Her argument that Romeo may never return to Verona and therefore will allow Juliet to marry Paris is absolutely unconvincing and a sign of her inability to distinguish between sex and love.

| p. 87 | What is Juliet's decision as far as the Nurse is concerned? |

The Nurse's 'advice' to forget Romeo and marry Paris has abruptly ended Juliet's trust in the Nurse's ability to help her solve her problem. Juliet becomes aware of the Nurse's low moral standard. She feels lonesome in this moment. There remains only one person she can confide in – and that is Friar Laurence.

Activities

| Anticipating grim fate p. 88 | At the end of this scene Juliet must come to terms with the fact that two people have 'deserted' her.
1. Why is she doubtful about seeing Romeo again? |

Is her uneasiness a result of an 'inner voice' or does she have a plausible reason for her doubts? – Juliet voices her doubt about seeing Romeo again for the very first time. This gnawing doubt may be a sign of her fear that the feud between the two families will pose an obstacle to their love, especially as she does not know how long Romeo's banishment from Verona will last.

2. Why is she determined to get rid of her nurse?

Let's not forget that a 14-year-old girl speaks to us in a way that even much older women of today wouldn't do.
The Nurse has helped Juliet in her attempt to get Romeo to church in time. She has defended her against her father's wrath, but she seems to act in this serious matter as if Juliet's marriage to Romeo has been a youthful transgression. She exhibits a behaviour that Juliet is not willing to tolerate. Juliet is deeply disappointed with the Nurse's way of thinking that she comes to the conclusion that she must solve her problems alone. In short, the Nurse can no longer be her confidante because the unswerving loyalty she has shown to Juliet so far has abruptly come to an end.

3. Continue writing her diary. What will she write down as soon as Romeo has secretly left her room?

Dear Diary,

Shall I weep, shall I cry, shall I jump for joy? – I don't know; my heart is broken – Romeo, my Romeo has gone – banished; he's left for Mantua – my husband, my lover – can I look to the future happily? – heaven knows the answer. What may this morning have in store for me? Paris wants me to become his wife. Angels in heaven, what can I do make the best of this desperate situation? My only hope will be the holy man, Friar Laurence – I am sure he will help me; will he…?

Both, Romeo and Juliet, complain about being victims of 'fickle fortune'.

◀ **The wheel of fortune p. 88**

1. Find out what 'fortune' meant to Elizabethan people.

Apart from what has been said about the goddess Fortuna (cf. answer to question on p. 82) more information can be found on page 142 of the students' book. Roland M. Frye adds the following lines: Referring to the Earl of Warwick's words in *Henry VI, Part 3,* (Act 5,

Scene 2, ll. 21–28) he writes: "Though Warrick does not explicitly mention Fortune's wheel in this speech, his remarks are closely related to the famous picture of the mythical goddess Fortune incessantly turning the wheel which foolish mortals insist upon riding: as the wheel turns, it raises one man towards the skies, just as it casts another into the mire ... it was also thought of as one of the major concerns of tragedy. It can be traced in almost all of Shakespeare's tragedies, as the protagonist is carried from felicity to misery and death." (*Shakespeare – the art of the dramatist,* London: Allen & Unwin, 1982, pp. 103–104).

2. Fortune then, astrology today – it's all the same, isn't it? Discuss.

This may be a help for the student's discussion:
"Form of *Divination* based on the theory that movements of the celestial bodies (stars, planets, Sun, and Moon) influence human affairs and determine events ... The spread of astrological practice was arrested by the rise of *Christianity,* with its emphasis on divine intervention and free will; but in the *Renaissance* astrology regained popularity, in part due to rekindled interest in science and *Astronomy.* Christian theologians warred against astrology, and in 1585 Sixtus V. condemned it. At the same time the work of *Kepler* and others undermined astrology's tenets, although the practice has continued. One's horoscope is a map of the heavens at the time of one's birth, showing the positions of the heavenly bodies in the ZODIAC." (THE LONGMAN ENCYCLOPEDIA, ed. Asa Briggs, London, 1989, p. 65).
It is Romeo himself who mentions the stars, cf. Act 1, Scene 4, l. 107: "some consequence yet hanging in the stars".
Why do people today believe in astrology? What is this a sign of? These are questions that may be at the core of the students's discussion.

Writing a sketch ▶ p. 88

Romeo meets his friend, Benvolio, and talks about his problems after killing Tybalt. Write a sketch in which they discuss the problem and come
1. to an agreement about how to tackle the problem of his secret marriage;

Place: near Verona, a hideaway known to both of them.

Romeo: Thanks for coming, Ben, this is something I would like to tell you, *only* you! You know this young lady, Juliet Capulet?

Benvolio: Yeah, this girl you were dancing with at the Capulets' feast on Sunday night!

Romeo: Right you are, and this is for *your eyes* only: We're married – secretly, you know. Friar Laurence did the job!

Benvolio: Wow, married!! I think you only had eyes for Rosaline! I won't believe it ... You really ...

Romeo: Come on, pull yourself together and listen to my plan: I've got to live in Mantua for the next few months. Friar

Act Three 55

Romeo: Laurence will help me smuggle Juliet out of Verona so that we can live together in Mantua. Will you support him in this matter?

Benvolio: You bet, I will. You can always count on me, buddy …

Romeo: I knew I could rely on you. Please go to the Friar's cell and tell him that I've met you and that you will lend us a hand; he will be glad to hear the news. Tell him I'm on my way to Mantua. He knows where I will be staying for the next few days.

Benvolio: O.K., that's fine; remember, I will come and see you in Mantua, be sure of that …

Romeo: Great, Ben, I am looking forward to seeing you … Bye, then.

Benvolio: See you soon, pal …!

2. to differing views in the end.

Romeo: … same text to: Will you support him in this matter?

Benvolio: Do you really think you will succeed in smuggling her out? I'm very doubtful about it, the guardsmen keep a close eye on all those people leaving Verona. Are you sure the Friar will help you? Wouldn't it be better if I went to the Prince and asked him to shorten the period of your exile?

Romeo: I'm a bit disappointed with you. I didn't think you would react that way …Well, then, let's stop pursuing the matter. But promise to keep your mouth shut about everything I told you …

Benvolio: That goes without saying! Nobody will hear a word from me, don't you worry …

Romeo: All right, then. God knows, when we will see each other again …

Write a film script of this scene. Cut all the lines which you think are not necessary for understanding the inherent problems of this scene. Compare the results with your classmates. Make a camcorder recording of the best version.

◀ **Shooting a script p. 88**

Teachers will best work with the *Romeo and Juliet* edition published by Hodder Children's Books, edited by Craig Pearce and Baz Luhrmann, London: 1996, pp. 122–132.
They can either copy the whole scene or part of it and then form two groups in the classroom to write their own film script with the help of this edition. Pearce and Luhrmann have cut the text a great deal for this film version, starring Leonardo Dicaprio and Claire Danes. The class will have to decide which words of Shakespeare's text they want to use and which should be left out.

Reviewing Act Three

Tybalt – a gentleman?
p. 88

Write Tybalt's obituary for a newspaper of the serious press.

The Verona Times
July 25 1597

Tybalt P. Sacchi made his name as the leader of a group called 'the caretakers' who made it their task to look after law and order in Verona – an outstanding achievement for a young man of 18 who began to care for our community early in his life.

Born in 1579 he very soon learned that money and honour were two ideals worth pursuing. His father's brother, the well-known Pierro D. Sacchi, introduced him at the age of ten, to our highly respected Prince Escalus, thus advancing his career as a very young activist in the service of our close-knit community.

Yesterday, Tybalt's promising career was brutally ended by a highly unfortunate accident. The blazing sun shone onto Cathedral Square when the unexpected happened: Mercutio met Tybalt and – nobody knows exactly who was to blame for it – started quarrelling. Tybalt fatally wounded Mercutio. He was terribly shocked, he told our correspondent later. When he returned to Cathedral Place to offer his condolences to Mercutio's friends he was waylaid by young Romeo Montague and killed in a fierce sword battle. Although a young supporter of the Montague family, Benvolio Stupidiano, asserted that Romeo was right in killing Tybalt, our revered Prince exiled Romeo at once. Justice was done. Tybalt, on the other hand, will be buried in the family monument tomorrow.

Honouring a deceased VIP
p. 88

You are a reporter for BBC Radio 4. You have to broadcast Mercutio's funeral service and the ceremony from the cathedral to the cemetry. Write the transcript of this broadcast. Don't forget that Mercutio is a very important person of the establishment because he is the Prince's relative.

This is Radio 4. We will now broadcast the funeral ceremony of Mercutio Escalus which is now under way. The requiem mass has just ended and our reporter, Benito Calzoni, will accompany the funeral procession from the Cathedral to the cemetry. Before we go over to Cathedral Square we would like to apologize to our listeners that the scheduled programme 'Any Questions' will be postponed until tomorrow. And now we cross over to Cathedral Square, calling our reporter Benito Calzoni.

Calzoni: Good morning and welcome to Cathedral Square, this place that has seen so many festive occasions in Verona, but today the atmosphere is different. People have come to say good-bye to one of the closest relatives of our Prince, Mercutio Escalus. Cathedral Square is crammed with onlookers watching Mercutio's coffin being carried from here to the city's cemetry at Flamingo Hill…

The students can be asked to continue this exercise in partner work. It will be at the students' discretion to add details of Mercutio's life as they wish. The reporter may have one of Mercutio's friends at his side who may help him draw a very vivid picture of the deceased as long as the procession is on its way to the cemetry.

Two citizens saw the youngsters fighting each other. A reporter from the local radio station asks them to voice their opinions about the feud between the two houses of Capulet and Montague (group work).

◄ **Voicing the common man's opinion p. 88**

Reporter: Good morning, ladies and gentlemen. This is Radio Verona: Today we have the opportunity in our series "Speak your mind" to welcome two members of our community with whom we can discuss the events which happened in Cathedral Square yesterday afternoon. First of all, I would like to address Signior Fulvio, one of the greengrocers, who sells his products in Cathedral Square every day. Signior Fulvio, do you remember how this quarrel started?
Fulvio: Well, you know, these youngsters with their green or blue jackets meet in Cathedral Square every day. As I say, they hang around there the whole day, these rich good-for-nothings …
Reporter: I see your point, Signior Fulvio. But what happened yesterday?
Fulvio: As I say, these rich good-for-nothings hang around the Place when suddenly a group of 'blue jackets' came onto the square and started a row with Mercutio, our Prince's nephew. I think the leader of this group, Tybalt, had shouted something in Mercutio's ears. In no time, they were duelling and then Mercutio shouted 'Outch' and was quickly carried away by two other blokes in green. A few minutes later we heard one of them shouting 'Mercutio's dead', and then 'Revenge for Mercutio's death'. Well, there was this dark-haired boy, this Romeo, well Paolo, you saw things better than I did, so you better carry on …
Reporter: As a matter of fact, ladies and gentlemen, let me introduce to you Signior Paolo Flavius; he's the other witness of yesterday's events. Signior Flavius, what can you add to Signior Fulvio's story?
Flavius: Indeed, Sir, I was just approaching Fulvio's market stall when this duel began. I heard this youngster, Romeo, crying out to Tybalt: "You killed my friend, you bloody old bugger … Well, if you ask me, these youngsters have a very rude way of addressing each other…
Reporter: You may be right, Signior Flavius, but how did this quarrel come to an end?
Flavius: This Romeo, well, he was so furious that Tybalt had no chance of leaving Cathedral Square alive. He really went mad and suddenly there was Tybalt on the ground, dead. Some of the bystanders shouted: "Romeo, away, away … if the Prince's guard gets hold of you they will throw you into prison". If you ask me, these blues and greens are a disgrace to our community. When will the Prince enforce the law so that these brawls cannot happen again? I wonder …
Reporter: Well, that's a good question to end our discussion. If you, dear listeners, would like to voice your views on this matter, phone us on o8oo 73 45 73 free of charge. Thanks for listening! Tune in to our next discussion of 'Speak your mind' in a fortnight. For now, goodbye and cheerio.

Giving the press some inside information
p. 89

Rosaline is interviewed by a reporter of the yellow press about her relationship with Romeo. What will she tell him now that she knows that Romeo has killed Tybalt, who is a distant relative of hers? (partner work)

Reporter: Hello, Rosaline, welcome to my office here at the "Verona Star". Our readers will be highly interested to hear from you what kind of person this Romeo Montague is. To start with, how well did you know him?
Rosaline: I knew him rather intimately, but do not get me wrong – not that intimately, as you might think …
Reporter: Our readers are keen on getting as much information as possible, you know we are the best-selling paper in Verona. So tell me, on how intimate terms was he with you, did he try to seduce you?
Rosaline: Well, maybe that was his intention. But I knew how to handle him. He behaved rather immaturely, bubbling over with enthusiasm when he saw me; in the end he got on my nerves – quoting poems and so on; telling me that he had written them for my eyes only. Terrible, behaved like a fool, a silly old fool.
Reporter: That's why you gave him the brush-off?
Rosaline: Well, that was one reason. The other thing was that he was never on time. Whenever we had a date he always arrived late, sometimes more than twenty minutes! Do you like people who are like that? I don't.
Reporter: Anything else, Rosaline? Your story could make the front page …
Rosaline: How many lira would I get if I gave you more details?
Reporter: Well, Rosaline, that depends on how closely we can work together …
Rosaline: You are just a filthy pig like all these other men who wanted to work together with me. Don't forget I am a virgin and I have no intention of losing my virginity with you. I have pledged to the Goddess Diana to remain chaste until I die. So don't insult me by offering me money for my virginity in return. I hope I never see you again, you womanizer …

(The last part of this 'interview' was left out in the newspaper article that appeared a day later – for understandable reason).

Alternative:

Rosaline: I don't care about being talked about on the front page. I may be gossipy but I wouldn't be so mean as to tell you something I know about Romeo only to ridicule him.
Reporter: Thanks for giving us a piece of your mind. Our readers will appreciate what you said about your relationship with Romeo Montague.

Gossiping in the market place
p. 89

The Nurse meets friends in the market place while doing some shopping. She is angry about old Capulet's behaviour towards her. Nevertheless, she and her friends agree that Juliet will make a good match when she marries Paris. What advantages concerning Paris will they especially boast of ? (group work)

Nurse: Hello, Giovanna, hello Paola, how are you? Still angry with your husband, Giovanna?

Giovanna: Tut, tut, Angelica, that's none of your business. Why do you look so frustrated?
Nurse: Ah, my master, Lord Capulet, he gives me the creeps these days; I don't know what has happened to him: Last night he went berserk, he almost killed his daughter, lovely Juliet. And you know why? He ordered her to marry Paris …
Paola: Paris, eh? And she refused to obey her father? Well, why didn't Capulet ask me? What a man, Paris! Wonderful, good-looking, chivalrous …
Giovanna: And rich he is, lives in a house, I say, in a palace, a superb garden and a little lake behind his house. Oh, how I would like to go swimming there, but I am married … He is such a good match! She would marry a fortune. You agree, Angelica, don't you?
Nurse: Of course, I do. He is a man of wax I told my sweet little Juliet yesterday, but she is mar… merry, so merry, being alone.
Paola: Well, Angelica, you are a good influence on her, tell her she could not get a better husband.
Nurse: Right you are, Paola, But go and tell her yourself, I wonder if you'll succeed …

Friar Laurence wants to support Romeo as much as possible. He writes a letter to a friend of his, a monk in Mantua, in which he asks him to help Romeo in his attempt to come to terms with his problems in his new surroundings. Write this letter.

◄ **Asking for spiritual support**
p. 89

Verona, 25/ 7 / 1597

Benedicte, Brother Francesco!

Our Lord Jesus has placed a heavy burden on me: One of my confidants, Romeo, son of Lord Montague killed Tybalt Sacchi in revenge for his fatally wounding Romeo's friend, Mercutio Escalus. Our highly-esteemed Prince Escalus, uncle to Mercutio, had to act quickly: Although Romeo had disobeyed his order for peace he understood that Romeo was not the first to have broken the law. That was the reason why Romeo did not receive a death sentence but was banished instead. He will have to leave for Mantua tomorrow early in the morning and will have to live there until we have succeeded in convincing the Prince to reverse his verdict. Brother Francesco, it is not only that I ask you to help Romeo to settle down in Mantua, but also to give him your spiritual support as there is another problem: Romeo was married to Juliet, daughter to Lord Capulet only three hours before these tragic accidents happened. I performed the wedding ceremony with the best intentions of helping the two families who are on very bad terms with each other. You will therefore understand what it means to Romeo not only to leave Verona but also his young wife. Please do everything in your power to give Romeo the support he needs in order to feel at home in Mantua. God bless you and Romeo.

Your spiritual brother
Laurence

P.S. Please drop me line as soon as Romeo has arrived in Mantua and let me know how he is getting on.

Act Four

> **Start here**

A terrible loss – or "how sour sweet music is"
p. 90

"If music be the food of love, play on." – If not, what then…? Discuss.

Three points require some comment and explanation here: (1) the sources of the quotations, (2) the role of music in *Romeo and Juliet,* and (3) the relationship between music and love in general.

Both quotations are from Shakespeare. The first one is from *King Richard II* (Act 5, Scene 5), while the second one is from *Twelfth Night* (Act 1, Scene 1). "The food of love" has become something of a cliché in modern English. Thus, for instance, in the ninth chapter of Jane Austen's *Pride and Prejudice,* Darcy says: "I have been used to consider poetry as the food of love."

In *Romeo and Juliet,* the role assumed by music is relatively modest, though by no means unimportant. In Act 2, Scene 5, music appears in one of Juliet's metaphors:

> Now, good sweet Nurse – O Lord, why look'st thou sad?
> Though news be sad, yet tell them merrily;
> If good, thou shamest the music of sweet news
> By playing it to me with so sour a face.

In Act 2, Scene 6 music is associated directly with love. Romeo and Juliet meet at a masked ball, and when Juliet returns Romeo's kiss, the young man says:

> Ah, Juliet, if the measure of thy joy
> Be heaped like mine, and that thy skill be more
> To blazon it, then sweeten with thy breath
> This neighbour air, and let rich music's tongue
> Unfold the imagined happiness that both
> Receive in either by this dear encounter.

In Act 4, Scene 4 Count Paris, accompanied by a group of musicians, approaches Capulet's house. As in Act 2, Scene 5, the link between music and love is evident, for Paris is coming to wed Juliet.

Finally, in Act 4, Scene 5, Paris arrives with his musicians. Since Juliet appears to be dead, the Capulets, who have been making arrangements for her wedding, decide to commence preparations for her funeral. The nuptial songs which were to have been sung during the marriage ceremony now have to be replaced by dirges:

> All things that we ordained festival,
> Turn from their office to black funeral:

> Our instruments to melancholy bells,
> Our wedding cheer to a sad burial feast;
> Our solemn hymns to sullen dirges change;
> Our bridal flowers serve for a buried corse;
> And all things change them to the contrary.

The latter part of the scene consists of a conversation between Peter and the musicians. Peter tries to persuade the men to play a tune called 'Heart's ease'.

Music is often associated with love, not only in works of literature, but also in real life. A typical literary example is provided by Thomas Mann's *Tonio Kröger*. As an adolescent, Tonio falls in love with one of his schoolmates – a boy called Hans Hansen, and later on he seeks to win the affection of a girl called Ingeborg Holm. In chapter VIII, as a sad and lonely young man, he watches Hans Hansen dancing with Ingeborg Holm, and there is a poignant contrast between the gaiety of the dance music and the sadness felt by Tonio.

In real life music and love are often inseparable – at least in Europe, where there is no taliban regime. People go to discos to look for partners, and they often listen to music while making love.

Act 4 Scene 1

Assignments

While-reading tasks

Do you think Paris's explanation is satisfactory? ◀ p. 91

The explanation offered by Paris is more ingenious than convincing. Paris argues that the marriage must be celebrated as soon as possible in order to assuage Juliet's passionate grief at Tybalt's death. However, although Juliet refers to Tybalt as her 'dear-loved cousin' (Act 3, Scene 2), she has evidently been more deeply affected by Romeo's banishment than by Tybalt's demise.

How may Juliet react to Paris greeting her? ◀ p. 91

She might retort that she has no intention of marrying Paris, but her actual reply is much more tactful.

Why is Juliet's answer 'him' ambiguous? ◀ p. 92

The pronoun *him* is ambiguous because it could refer to Romeo as well as to Paris. Paris fails to perceive this ambiguity because he assumes that both *you* and *him* refer to himself.

p. 92 ▶ What does Juliet refer to?

When Juliet says 'It may be so', she means 'I may have vilified my face'. When she says 'it is not mine own', she means that her face belongs to someone else. She is referring to Romeo, but Paris imagines she is referring to himself.

p. 92 ▶ Why is Friar Laurence at a loss at this moment?

The monk is at a loss what to do next because Capulet and Paris have reached an agreement and he can suggest no means whereby Juliet's marriage to the Count might be delayed or prevented.

p. 92 ▶ What is Juliet willing to do?

She is prepared to attempt suicide if Friar Laurence cannot help her.

p. 93 ▶ How does Juliet express her disgust at the idea of marrying Paris?

Juliet expresses her abhorrence in a highly rhetorical speech which reveals her morbid sensibility. She enumerates various actions which she says she would consider preferable to a marriage with Paris. All the actions in question are terrifying or repulsive: jumping from the battlements of a tower, walking along lanes haunted by thieves, lying under a pile of skeletons in a charnel house, sharing a shroud with a dead man, etc.

p. 93 ▶ How will the Friar prevent Juliet from marrying Paris?

In order to prevent the marriage, Friar Laurence will give Juliet a sleeping potion which will plunge her into a state of suspended animation.

Activities

A joyful event to come? ▶
p. 95

In this scene Paris appears very self-assured because he has Capulet's word that 'on Thursday next' Juliet will become his wife. He tries to settle things with Friar Laurence. And as it happens he also meets Juliet for the first time.

1. What may they have talked about before the scene begins? Write a short introductory sketch.

Paris: Good morning, Friar.
Friar Laurence: Bless me, Sir Paris! What brings you here at such an early hour?
Paris: Last night I had an important conversation with Lord Capulet.
Friar Laurence: I suppose you talked about the consequences of Tybalt's death.
Paris: No, we discussed something quite different, something which has nothing whatever to do with poor Tybalt's tragic and untimely death.
Friar Laurence: And what might that be?

Paris: A matter of the very deepest moment – at least for me. Lord Capulet has granted me his daughter's hand, and the wedding is to take place on Thursday.

2. What will he tell his friends about his meeting with Juliet?

Juliet's verbal sparring has no doubt made a strong impression on Paris, so he will probably tell his friends that the girl is both attractive and witty. He may add that she loves him, and that she has made no objections whatever to their forthcoming marriage.

3. How will he convey to them his delight at marrying such a beauty?

He will probably talk endlessly about Juliet's appearance.

Friar Laurence is, as a man of the Church, an authority. Why does he use a trick in order to get Juliet out of her troubles instead of openly speaking his mind to her parents?

◄ Lacking spiritual authority? p. 95

Friar Laurence probably resorts to a subterfuge because he believes there is no point in remonstrating with Capulet, who is a stern unbending man.

Act 4 Scene 2

Assignments

While-reading tasks

Why does Juliet apparently behave so obediently towards her father?

◄ p. 96

She feigns obedience to her father's wishes for two reasons. First, she knows she will incur her father's wrath if she wears her heart on her sleeve. Second, she is confident that she will eventually succeed in outwitting her parents.

Why does old Capulet seem to be in such a good mood?

◄ p. 96

Capulet is delighted because he imagines that he has succeeded in overcoming his daughter's resistance.

Why is Capulet's last sentence an example of 'dramatic irony'?

◄ p. 96

The term *dramatic irony* is generally applied to a situation which arises when a character in a play speaks lines which have for the audience a meaning not intended by the speaker. A good example is provided by the scene in Shakespeare's *Macbeth* (Act 2, Scene 3) where the drunken porter jestingly talks of being the porter at Hell's gate. In this particular instance, however, the situation is somewhat different. Capulet's words do not carry any extra meaning to the audience, but the audience knows Capulet is mistaken in thinking that his rebellious daughter has been won back to obedience.

Activities

To err is human ▶ p. 97

Juliet's obvious consent to marry Paris will strengthen the Nurse's opinion that she has given Juliet the right advice.
1. What will the Nurse say to her and what will Juliet answer as soon as they are in Juliet's room? Write down this short dialogue.

Nurse: Young lady, I'm so happy that you've followed my advice. Didn't I tell you there was no point in weeping over Romeo's banishment?
Juliet: You did indeed, my dear nurse.
Nurse: Didn't I tell you the wisest thing for you to do was to marry Paris?
Juliet: Yes, my dear nurse.
Nurse: Isn't Paris handsome, love?
Juliet: He's not an ugly man.
Nurse: Isn't he far more handsome than Romeo, love?
Juliet: I don't know what to answer, my dear nurse.

2. How does old Capulet behave during the preparations for the wedding? Discuss.

Capulet assists personally in the wedding preparations. Instead of going to bed, he performs a number of tasks which would normally be accomplished by a bride's mother.

Great ▶ expectations! p. 97

Two of Capulet's servants are in the marketplace buying a lot of things needed for the wedding. Write down what they may be thinking of this forthcoming ceremony.

Sampson: I wonder why old Capulet's in such a hurry to get his daughter married.
Gregory: So do I. Poor Tybalt's just been buried.
Sampson: I dare say Capulet's interested in Paris's money.
Gregory: Capulet doesn't need Paris's money. He's filthy rich.
Sampson: You mean it's all a question of social prestige?
Gregory: Yes, of course it is. Paris is related to the Prince.
Sampson: What about Juliet? Does she want to marry Paris?
Gregory: I've heard she's in love with Romeo.
Sampson: Upon my word! There'll be ructions if her father ever finds out.
Gregory: There'll be ructions if we don't get a move on. It's getting late, and we haven't yet bought half of the victuals old Capulet needs for the wedding reception.

Act 4 Scene 3

Assignments

While-reading tasks

Why does Juliet tell her nurse that she has led a sinful life? ◀ p. 97

She tells her nurse that she has led a sinful life because she wants to be alone. Friar Laurence has told her to make sure that she is alone when she swallows the potion he has prepared for her (Act 4, Scene 1), so she pretends she is going to spend the night praying for God's forgiveness.

What feelings does Juliet express here? ◀ p. 98

In this passage Juliet expresses her fear and anguish at the thought of forsaking the everyday world for a mysterious realm of which she knows nothing.

What is Juliet willing to do if the poison does not work? ◀ p. 98

If the poison does not work, Juliet is prepared to attempt suicide by stabbing herself.

Can you explain Juliet's strange behaviour here? ◀ p. 98

Juliet speaks and acts so strangely because she is deeply distraught. As she ponders over various aspects of her situation, all kinds of horrible fancies crowd upon her. She wonders whether Friar Laurence has given her a deadly poison, she imagines what might happen if she emerges from her coma before Romeo's arrival, and she even has a vision of her dead cousin.

Activities

In this scene Juliet is in agony in coming to terms with this desperate situation. ◀ Why does heaven not help? p. 99

1. Write a poem – why not a sonnet? – in which you try to express Juliet's hopes and fears.

It is advisable to remind pupils that there are four types of sonnet, viz. the Petrarchan sonnet, the Shakespearean sonnet, the Miltonic sonnet, and the Spenserian sonnet.

The Petrarchan sonnet is divided into two parts. The octave invariably rhymes *abbaabba,* while the sestet normally rhymes *cdecde.* The rhyme scheme of the sestet admits some variation, but there are never more than five rhymes in the poem.

The Shakespearean sonnet is divided into three quatrians and a concluding couplet. The rhyme scheme is usually *abab, cdcd, efef, gg*, or *abba, cddc, effe, gg*.

The Miltonic sonnet observes the octave rhyme scheme of the Petrarchan sonnet (*abba, abba*), but there is no pause at the beginning of the sestet, and the rhyme scheme of the sestet may take on a variety of forms.

The Spenserian sonnet (also known as the link sonnet), has a rhyme scheme which links octave and sestet, and concludes with a rhymed couplet: *abab, bcbc, cdcd, ee*.

The octave might be used to express Juliet's fears, while the rest of the poem might be given over to a depiction of her hopes.

2. How would you behave in such a critical situation? Discuss it in groups and try to find a solution to the problem.

Among other things, the teacher might remind pupils of the rules for conditional sentences and draw their attention to the numerous words and word groups that can be combined with nouns such as *dilemma*, e.g. *a fearful dilemma, a serious dilemma, to be in a dilemma, to face a dilemma, to resolve a dilemma, to extricate oneself from a dilemma, to place someone in a dilemma, to pose a dilemma for someone, to be reduced to the dilemma of* + GERUND, *a dilemma arises, there is no other way out of the dilemma*, etc.

3. In today's society a teenager like Juliet or Romeo would not ask advice from a nanny but would rather get in touch with an agony aunt. Write this letter.

A girl in Juliet's position might write a letter like this:

Dear Ms Hart,

I need your advice urgently because I'm in a terrible predicament.

My parents want me to marry a fella they've taken a fancy to. He's called Andrew, he comes from an aristocratic family, he's very well off, he has a posh accent, and he's quite good-looking. The trouble is he's never really turned me on. Frankly, I think I'd go completely round the bend if I had to go to bed with him every night for the rest of my life.

I'm not frigid or lesbian, or anything like that though, and I'm not indifferent to money either. You see, there's another guy – a young scrap merchant called Romeo. I met him only a few weeks ago at a masked ball, and when he put his arms round me and kissed me on the mouth I almost fainted. I'm not exaggerating. I'm madly in love with him, and he's crazy about me too.

Last week he climbed over the garden wall in the middle of the night. He threw pebbles on to my balcony to wake me, and when I opened the French window and came out in my transparent nightie, there he was, standing in the middle of the moonlit lawn like an apparition. It was ever so romantic!

Yesterday we went to see a priest called Father Laurence. Romeo gave him five quid, and the old codger married us secretly. This morning, however, my dad told me Andrew would be coming here next week to discuss the arrangements for our wedding. My parents take it for granted that I've no objection, and there'll be a blazing row if I tell them I've just got married to another bloke.

To make matters worse, my dad knows Romeo's dad, and he can't stand the sight of him. He's always slagging him off. He'll murder me if he finds out what's happened!

I'm up against a brick wall now. Do you think I ought to run away from home or just stay and face the music? Please help me.

Yours sincerely,
Juliet

A young man in Romeo's position might write a letter like this:

Dear Mr Moody,

I've decided to write to you because I'm in a jam.

I've just married a girl called Juliet, and we're absolutely crazy about each other. The trouble is we've had to get hitched secretly. You see, Juliet's dad wants his daughter to marry somebody else, and he'd never accept me as a son-in-law because my dad's his most hated enemy.

Juliet's dad's already started to make arrangements for his daughter's wedding. He wants her to marry some guy called Andrew. There'll be ructions if he finds out what's happened, and Juliet might even commit suicide.

I'm at my wit's end wondering how I'm going to sort out this mess. Please write soon and tell me what I ought to do. This business is driving me crackers.

Yours sincerely,
Romeo

4. Work in groups. Make cassette recordings of Juliet's soliloquy (lines 24–58). Compare the recordings, then award a prize to the best group and the best speaker.

Special attention should be given to details such as the dramatically extra-metrical quality of the last line.

Act 4 Scene 4

Assignments

While-reading tasks

p. 100 ▶ Why is Capulet staying up so late?

He is staying up late because he wants to supervise the preparations for Juliet's wedding.

Activities

Motherly feelings?
p. 101 ▶ Lady Capulet has withdrawn to her room for a short rest.

1. What thoughts may cross her mind at this moment?

She will probably think about Tybalt's tragic death, the arrangements for the wedding ceremony, Juliet's refusal to marry Paris, and the sudden, unexpected change in her attitude after her visit to Friar Laurence.

2. Is she looking forward to the wedding or may she be anticipating some unforeseeable events?

She may fear some untoward events if she is perspicacious enough to realise that Juliet's startling change of heart has been prompted by guile rather than by a sense of duty towards her parents.

3. Does this scene have any relevance to the progress of events in the play? Discuss.

Act 4 Scene 4 is superfluous since it overlaps with the last lines of Act 4 Scene 2 and the opening lines of Act 4 Scene 5. At the end of Act 4 Scene 2, Capulet says he is going to stay up all night in order to supervise the wedding preparations; and in Act 4 Scene 5 the Nurse arrives in Juliet's bedchamber and tries in vain to wake the sleeping girl.

Act 4 Scene 5

Assignments

While-reading tasks

p. 101 ▶ What makes the Nurse behave so happily?

The Nurse is in high spirits because she is looking forward to the wedding ceremony and she fails to realise that Juliet is in a state of suspended animation. She imagines that the girl has overslept.

Are Lady Capulet's feelings genuine? ◀ p. 102

The odds are that Lady Capulet's grief is not genuine, for in Act 3, Scene 5 she speaks contemptuously of her daughter, saying: 'I would the fool were married to her grave.'

Does Capulet exaggerate or is his grief sincere? ◀ p. 102

There are good grounds for thinking that his grief is not sincere, for his language is artificial and his brutal behaviour in Act 3 Scene 5 suggests that his affection for his daughter is only skin-deep.

Can we understand Paris's grief? ◀ p. 103

There are strong grounds for doubting the sincerity of Paris's grief since the young count barely knows Juliet.

How does the Friar try to comfort the family in their grief? ◀ p. 103

The Friar tries to comfort the family by claiming that Juliet is better off in heaven.

What is music good for according to Peter? ◀ p. 104

Peter believes that music can be an important source of comfort for the bereaved.

Why does Peter talk about such unimportant matters? ◀ p. 105

Peter evidently enjoys exchanging banter with the musicians. His jesting helps to assuage his sorrow, and it also provides comic relief for the audience.

Activities

Friar Laurence is the only person who knows the truth about the events that have occurred. ◀ Life's little ironies? p. 105

1. What is our reaction to his words about Juliet's happiness in heaven?
   Are they spoken convincingly?

If Friar Laurence is a good actor, his words may well be spoken convincingly, but this does not alter the fact that his arguments are specious. Besides, we know he cannot possibly be sincere because it was he who gave Juliet the concoction which is responsible for her apparent death.

2. How would you react if a joyous event turned into a tragic affair?

If a joyous event ended in tragedy, my reactions would depend to a large extent on whether I was directly involved. If the tragic events in question affected my friends or relatives, I would naturally be shocked and deeply saddened.

3. How may the Montagues have reacted to the news of Juliet's 'death' although they do not know anything about Romeo's secret marriage?
Write down this conversation between Lord and Lady Montague.

Lord Montague: Have you heard the news about Capulet's daughter?
Lady Montague: No. What's she done?
Lord Montague: I've no idea what she's done, but the servants say she's dead.
Lady Montague: Dead? Merciful heavens! She was to be married to Paris this morning. Has somebody killed her?
Lord Montague: According to the servants, she died in her sleep.
Lady Montague: How odd! I wonder if somebody's poisoned her.
Lord Montague: She may have poisoned herself.
Lady Montague: What makes you think that?
Lord Montague: Rumour has it that she had a violent argument with her father on Tuesday morning.
Lady Montague: What did they quarrel about?
Lord Montague: It appears they quarreled about Juliet's forthcoming marriage.
Lady Montague: Didn't Juliet want to marry Paris?
Lord Montague: The servants say she refused point-blank.
Lady Montague: Did she give any reasons for her refusal?
Lord Montague: Rumour has it that she was in love with another man.
Lady Montague: And who might that have been?
Lord Montague: Romeo.
Lady Montague: Romeo, our Romeo?
Lord Montague: I've no idea what Romeo's been up to, but he's been very secretive of late, and he was seen near Capulet's palace on Monday evening.

Curtains for the Nurse ▶ p. 106

This is the Nurse's last entry on the stage. Why do you think Shakespeare has made her exit from the play now?

At this point Shakespeare probably decided to eliminate the Nurse for two reasons. First, she is only a supporting character. Secondly, by the end of the fourth act she has already fulfilled the purpose for which she was created. Her comic prattling would have been inappropriate in Act 5, where the central characters die in particularly tragic circumstances.

Comic relief? ▶ p. 106

What may be the function of this rather inappropriate prattling by the musicians when they are told they should pack up their instruments?

This exchange serves to provide comic relief after the discovery of Juliet's apparently lifeless body.

Reviewing Act Four

A drink like that given to Juliet by Friar Laurence would not work today, according to modern medical knowledge.

1. How would you help Juliet prevent getting married a second time?

In order to enable Juliet to avoid a second marriage, I would try to smuggle her out of the country.

2. Do you think that a 14-year old girl would be so clever today as to be able to deceive a lot of people concerning her state of mind?

There seems little reason to assume that girls born in the second half of the twentieth century are less intelligent than their ancestors, so a modern 14-year old girl might well equal Juliet's performance if she were sufficiently resourceful and cool-headed.
In Western Europe, most parents are now very liberal, and they allow their children much more freedom than was usual in former times. Instead of debating the question of girls' intelligence teachers might therefore find it more profitable to discuss relationships between parents and children.

◀ **Helping a friend in need**
p. 106

Friar Laurence has promised to 'send a friar [...] to Mantua with my letters to thy lord.'

1. How many letters might that be?

At the end of Act 4 Scene 1, Friar Laurence twice refers to 'letters':

> In the mean time, against thou shalt awake,
> Shall Romeo by my letters know our drift,
> [...] I'll send a friar with speed
> To Mantua, with my letters to thy lord.

Similarly, in Act 5 Scene 1, Romeo, in his conversation with Balthasar, twice inquires about 'letters' from Friar Laurence:

> Dost thou not bring me letters from the friar?
> [...] Hast thou no letters to me from the friar?

The use of the plural, however, does not necessarily mean that Friar Laurence wrote more than one missive and that Romeo expected to receive more than one. In Zeffirelli's film, Friar Laurence sends only one letter to Romeo, and there are good grounds for believing that Zeffirelli's interpretation is correct:

- One letter is quite sufficient.
- In sixteenth-century English *letters*, like the Latin noun *litterae*, was sometimes used with singular meaning (cf. the quotation from *Othello* in the *O.E.D.*, s.v. *letter*).
- In Act 5 Scene 2, Friar Laurence uses the noun *letter* in the singular ('Who bare my letter, then, to Romeo?' / 'The letter was not nice [...]'), and *letter* without a plural ending cannot be a misprint here

◀ **Asking a colleague for support**
p. 106

since Friar Laurence and Friar John both repeatedly use the singular pronoun *it* to refer to the missive in question.
- In Act 5 Scene 3, Friar Laurence once more employs the noun *letter* in the singular ('he which bore my letter, Friar John').

At the end of Act 5 Scene 2, Friar Laurence says he is going to send a second letter to Romeo ('[…] I will write again to Mantua […]'), but Shakespeare makes no further mention of it.

2. What might their contents be? Work in groups and write these letters.

In modern English, Friar Laurence might have written something like this:

Dear Romeo,

When Juliet takes the powerful sleeping draught I have just made up for her, she will go into a resistant state of suspended animation. After remaining in this death-like state for forty two hours, she will awake as from a pleasant sleep. When Paris comes to wed her on Thursday morning, she will present the appearance of someone who has just died. There will be no sign of movement, no pulse, no breath, no beating of the heart. Her face will wear a waxen pallor, and her whole body will be cold and rigid. She will probably be buried in the accustomed manner in the Capulets' tomb.

If you return secretly to Verona late on Friday evening, you will find me waiting for you near the gates of the cemetery. We shall go to the Capulets' tomb, open the door with a crowbar, descend into the vault, and wait there until Juliet awakes. Then you can take her away to Mantua.

Despite the ingenuity of my plan, much could go awry. Even as I write this letter, myriads of horrible fancies begin to crowd in upon my mind. I trust to God that my fears are unfounded.

With best wishes,
Yours,

Friar Laurence

Lamenting a 'suicide' p. 106

All the members of the Capulet family know that Juliet has committed "suicide". There is a lot of lamenting over her death, nevertheless:

1. Who can really be held responsible?

There can be no doubt that Juliet's parents are to blame. If they had been less intransigent, the girl would not have been obliged to resort to the sleeping potion subterfuge.

2. Write a scene in which Hercule Poirot is working on the case trying to find an answer to this "suicide" by using his "little grey cells".

Let us assume that Poirot arrives on Friday morning, about 24 hours after Juliet's first funeral.

Hercule Poirot: Why do you think your daughter committed suicide, *madame*?
Lady Capulet: She didn't want to marry Count Paris, and we found an empty phial beside her body.
Hercule Poirot: You want to know who gave Juliet the phial in question, yes?
Lady Capulet: Precisely, Mr Poirot. The person who gave Juliet the phial of poison is a dangerous malefactor, and he – or she – must be punished.
Hercule Poirot: May I have a look at the phial, *madame*?
Lady Capulet: Here it is.
Hercule Poirot (*wrinkling up his nose and sniffing delicately at the phial*): I would not describe the smell as noisome, *madame*, but it is very odd, very odd indeed.
Lady Capulet: Can you identify the poison, Mr Poirot?
Hercule Poirot (*frowning*): It is quite unlike anything I have ever smelt in the course of my long career.
Lady Capulet: So you can't help.
Hercule Poirot: *Si, madame*. Me, I think we ought to pursue a fresh line of inquiry.
Lady Capulet: Could you be more specific, Mr Poirot?
Hercule Poirot: *Eh bien,* instead of trying to identify the decoction that was in the phial, we might try to identify the person who gave it to your daughter.
Lady Capulet: That will be exceedingly difficult, Mr Poirot. You see, we have scores of servants and …
Hercule Poirot: You think one of the servants might be the culprit, yes?
Lady Capulet: I don't know what to think. I can't make head nor tail of this shocking affair.
Hercule Poirot: It is exceptionally difficult, this problem, but I am persuaded that I shall be able to resolve it. Let me think, *madame*. My little grey cells are *en émoi*. (*He pauses for a moment.*) Me, I think I know how to proceed now. Tell me, is there anyone in your household who had a particularly close relationship with your daughter?
Lady Capulet: Yes, of course. The Nurse. But surely you don't …
Hercule Poirot: Me, I think it is very unwise to jump to conclusions, *madame*. Tell me, *madame*, what kind of a person is the Nurse?
Lady Capulet: A very foolish and garrulous woman.
Hercule Poirot: *Eh bien,* if she is as garrulous as you say, it is possible that she will be able to set us on the right track.
Lady Capulet: Would you like to speak to her alone or in my presence?
Hercule Poirot: You may remain here if you wish, *madame*.
Lady Capulet (*calling out in a loud and imperious voice*): Nurse! Come here at once!

Enter Nurse.

Nurse: Did you call me, Madam?
Lady Capulet: Nurse, this is Mr Poirot, a famous detective who is investigating Juliet's untimely death. Mr Poirot wishes to ask you a few questions.

Nurse: Good morning, sir. What would you like to know, sir?
Hercule Poirot: Good morning, Nurse. You discovered Juliet's body in her bedchamber, yes?
Nurse: Yes, sir, that's perfectly true. (*She begins to weep and wipes her eyes with her apron.*) That was yesterday morning, sir. It was really awful, sir. She was lying on her back with her eyes closed, and she was as white as a sheet. You can't imagine how awful it was, sir.
Hercule Poirot: I am sure you were very distressed. But I would like to ask you about something else.
Nurse: Yes, sir.
Hercule Poirot: Did you see anything unusual on the bed or on the floor beside the bed?
Nurse: No sir, I didn't. I only saw poor Juliet, sir. Oh, you can't imagine how awful it was to see that poor child lying there all stiff and cold. (*She begins to weep again.*)
Lady Capulet: I was the one who discovered the phial, Mr Poirot.
Hercule Poirot (*holding up the phial*): Tell me, Nurse, does this receptacle remind you of anything you have seen elsewhere in this house?
Nurse (*wiping her eyes and peering at the phial*): I'm not sure, sir.
Hercule Poirot: It is made of dark brown glass, and there is a little cross on it.
Nurse (*her eyes widening in surprise*): Oh yes, sir. You're right. I hadn't noticed the little cross. Let me think. (*She pauses and wipes her nose with her apron.*) It reminds me of a phial I got from Friar Laurence a few months ago. You see, I had a bad cold, and Friar Laurence gave me a cough mixture. It was in a phial that looks just like the one you're holding in your hand.
Hercule Poirot (*turning to Lady Capulet*): Who is Friar Laurence, *madame*?
Lady Capulet: An old monk who lives near here. He's very knowledgeable about plants.
Hercule Poirot: *Tiens, tiens.* How very interesting! Me, I think I ought to interview Friar Laurence. I am persuaded that he will be able to shed some light on the mystery you have asked me to solve.

Hercule Poirot uses a kind of interlanguage – a rather exotic mixture of English and French, interspersed with elements that are neither French nor English. The following points require some comment and explanation:

- Poirot addresses Lady Capulet as *madame*. A native speaker of English would have said *my lady*. Cf. Oscar Wilde, *A Woman of No Importance:* 'Mrs. Arbuthnot's compliments, my lady, but she has a bad headache, and cannot see anyone this morning.'
- The adverb *si* is used here in the same way as the German word *doch*. *Si, madame* could be rendered as *Yes I can, my lady*.
- *Eh bien* corresponds to *well*.
- *En émoi* could be translated as *in turmoil*. *My mind is in turmoil* would be normal English, but Poirot always talks about his 'little grey cells'.
- *Tiens, tiens!* would be *Well, well!* in English.
- On several occasions Poirot uses *yes* as a question tag because he imagines it corresponds to *n'est-ce pas?* or *non* in end position. The

interrogative sentences ending in *yes* could be reformulated as follows: *You want to know who gave Juliet the phial in question, don't you? You think one of the servants might be the culprit, don't you? You discovered Juliet's body in her bedchamber, didn't you?* or *I understand that you discovered Juliet's body in her bedchamber.*
- *Me, I* is a literal translation of *Moi, je.* Since Poirot's knowledge of English grammar is rather patchy, he imagines that the disjunctive pronoun *moi* corresponds to *me*. In order to correct the sentences beginning with *Me, I,* we have to omit the pronoun *me*.
- *It is exceptionally difficult, this problem* is a literal translation of the French sentence *Il est exceptionellement difficile, ce problème,* where dislocation, designed to bring the noun *problème* into a strong position, involves a duplication of the subject (*il, problème*). Poirot ought to have said: *This problem is exceptionally difficult.* We might add that the type of syntactic dislocation under discussion is also possible in English, although it is much less common in English than in French. Good examples are provided by the following sentences: 'Look, is <u>it</u> really so important to you, <u>the affair with Caroline</u>, even if it is true?' (P. D. James, *Devices and Desires*); '<u>They</u> were all fitting into place, <u>the jig-saw pieces</u>.' (D. Du Maurier, *Rebecca*).
- *I am persuaded that [...]* is a literal translation of the French syntagma *je suis persuadé que [...]*. Poirot should have said: *I am convinced that [...]*.
- *It is possible that [...]* is grammatically correct, but Poirot tends to overuse this construction because he imagines it is the only English equivalent of *il est possible que [...]* and *il se peut que [...]*. In modern English, however, the best equivalents of these constructions are often *may, might* or *maybe*. Poirot should therefore have said *she may be able to set us on the right track,* instead of *it is possible that she will be able to set us on the right track.*
- Finally, it should be noted that Poirot, like many non-native speakers of English, consistently avoids colloquial contractions. Thus, for instance, he says *I would not* instead of *I wouldn't* and *it is* instead of *it's*.

3. In his film version of Romeo and Juliet, Franco Zeffirelli has left out scene 4 and most of scene 5. Do you think they are important for understanding the rest of the play?

In a modern performance, Scene 4 would be quite superfluous since the information it conveys is deducible from the final lines of Act 4 Scene 2 and the opening lines of Act 4 Scene 5. However, one should never forget that Elizabethan stage practice was quite different from ours. In Shakespare's day, the scene in question may well have served a useful purpose by enabling some of the actors to gain time if they still had to make some preparations behind the scenes.

Unlike Scene 4, Scene 5 is important for two reasons:

- Its first part is potentially very dramatic.
- It shows us how the Capulets react to Juliet's apparent death.

The main weak points of the scene are its excessive length, its tedious repetitions, and its florid language. A few examples will suffice:

- Friar Laurence's long-winded arguments (lines 65–83) could be reduced to three or four lines.
- The conversation between Peter and the musicians is rather boring and not really necessary, although it does provide some comic relief.
- Lady Capulet and the Nurse say more or less the same things in lines 23–24 and lines 43–54.
- The speeches are full of bombast. Paris and Capulet, for instance, reel off absurdly long strings of past participles and apostrophise life, death and time in turgid verse.

Zeffirelli's version, by contrast, is masterly. The camera pans slowly up the outer walls of Capulet's palace; then a piercing shriek rends the morning air. Clad in a white nightgown, the Nurse rushes out of Juliet's bedchamber and leans over a balcony, wailing and weeping hysterically. Aroused by the Nurse's screams, Lord and Lady Capulet hasten to their daughter's room. Their lamentations, which extend over more than 30 lines in Shakespeare's text, are reduced to an absolute minimum. At the sight of Juliet's apparently lifeless body, Lord Capulet exclaims:

> O lamentable day!
> Death lies on her like an untimely frost
> Upon the sweetest flower of all the field.

'O lamentable day!' corresponds to line 29 in the original, where it is spoken by the Nurse. The other lines, which are deeply moving, correspond to lines 28–29 in Shakespeare's text.

Act Five

Start here

"Well, Juliet, I will lie with thee tonight." – What is your understanding of this sentence?

▸ **Who is to blame?** p. 107

These words are spoken by Romeo in Act 5, Scene 1. In his despair, the young man decides to break into Juliet's burial vault and die over her corpse. He makes a macabre pun on the verb <u>lie</u>, which in Shakespearean English can have two entirely different meanings when it is followed by the preposition <u>with</u> and a noun or pronoun denoting a person: (1) to lie dead, and (2) to have sexual intercourse. This wordplay, which creates a link between love and death, serves to underline the poignancy of the situation.

Act 5 Scene 1

Assignments

While-reading tasks

What news does Balthasar convey to Romeo?

▸ p. 108

Balthasar tells Romeo that Juliet has died and been buried in the Capulets' tomb.

Why does Romeo describe the Apothecary in such detail?

▸ p. 109

He gives an extremely detailed description of the Apothecary in order to convey a vivid impression of the man's poverty. It is important that the audience should be aware of the Apothecary's penny because the man would have refused to sell his poison if he had not been so short of money.

Activities

How does Romeo react to the news given to him by Balthasar?

▸ **Conveying a delicate message** p. 111

1. Do you think he is crying, shouting or is he reacting calmly? In your answer do not forget that he spoke of 'joyful news' only a minute before Balthasar's entrance.

His mood changes abruptly. He is evidently distraught, for Balthasar says: 'Your looks are pale and wild, and do import / Some misadventure.'

2. If you had been in Balthasar's place, how would you have conveyed this rather sad news to Romeo?

I would have tried to break the news gradually.

3. Do you think the dialogue with the Apothecary is absolutely necessary? Write a monologue of about ten lines in which Romeo tells the audience that he wants to acquire poison in order to die with Juliet.

The dialogue with the Apothecary is not absolutely necessary. It could be replaced by a brief statement by Romeo to the effect that he intends to purchase some deadly poison before returning to Verona. We might add that Zeffirelli, who cuts Shakespeare's text very heavily, omits the dialogue with the Apothecary altogether.

Romeo's monologue might read as follows:

How bleak and dismal everything seems now! All of a sudden my life's lost all meaning. I've never experienced anything like this before. This grief, this aching emptiness, this suffering's unbearable. I can't go on like this. I simply can't go on living without Juliet. I've no choice but to put an end to my life… Yes, that's what I'll do. I'll kill myself. When I'm dead I won't suffer any more, and I might even be reunited with Juliet in some shadowy world where disembodied spirits can communicate with one another… I'll go to Juliet's tomb and kill myself there… Now what's the best way to commit suicide? Should I stab myself? No, that's too messy. Besides, I might lose consciousness as soon as the blade cuts into my flesh, and somebody might find me and fetch a doctor. There must be something better… I know what! I'll poison myself. I'll go and see that half-starved apothecary I met yesterday. His shop's not far from here. If I offer him enough money he'll give me the most potent poison he has.

Act 5 Scene 2

Assignments

While-reading task

p. 112 ▶ Why must Friar Laurence go to the Capulets' monument?

Friar Laurence has to go to the tomb because Juliet is going to emerge from her coma shortly.

Activities

Letter to Mantua – but how? p. 112 ▶ The letter to Romeo was not delivered, but "I will write again to Mantua", says Friar Laurence.

1. How will he manage to send the letter to Romeo this time? Discuss possible suggestions.

He might get in touch with one of Romeo's friends. Benvolio, for instance, would certainly be prepared to take the letter to Mantua.

2. The letter could not reach Romeo because the health officers did not allow Friar John to leave Verona for fear of possible infections.
Write a short dialogue involving the officers and the monks; the friars try to convince the officers that nobody has to fear anything and that they urgently have to leave town.

First Officer: Stop! You can't leave the city.
Friar John: But we must go to Mantua.
Second Officer: You were in a house where a man has just died of the plague.
Friar Matthew: That's not true.
Friar John: We can prove that we never went near any houses where people were suffering from the plague.
First Officer: Shut up. We're not going to waste our time arguing with you. Go into that house on the left. The door's ajar.
Friar John: Look, we've got to deliver a letter. It's urgent.
Second Officer: You've got to stay here. If you leave Verona, you'll spread the plague everywhere.
Friar Matthew: Will you allow us to entrust the letter to someone else?
First Officer: That's out of the question. The letter may be contaminated.

Act 5 Scene 3

Assignments

While-reading tasks

Is Paris's love for Juliet genuine or only make-believe? ◀ p. 113

It is hard to decide whether Paris's love for Juliet is genuine. In this scene, he seems to be overwhelmed with grief, yet he never had a close relationship with Juliet, and his behaviour in the first part of the play is rather odd. In Act 1, Scene 2 he expresses interest in Juliet and is invited by Capulet to attend a feast where he will have ample opportunities to compare Juliet with other marriageable girls. In Act 1, Scene 5, however, Paris is conspicuous by his absence.

How will Balthasar reply to Romeo's threatening words? ◀ p. 114

He acquiesces meekly and walks away in order not to anger his master, then he hides near the tomb to watch.

What does Romeo address? ◀ p. 114

He addresses the tomb as if it were a person.

p. 115	**How does Romeo speak these words, calmly or agitatedly?**
	Romeo no doubt speaks in great agitation.
p. 115	**Who is meant by "my man"?**
	'My man' refers to Romeo's servant, Balthasar.
p. 116	**Why is Romeo fatally mistaken here?**
	Romeo is mistaken because he is convinced that Juliet is dead.
p. 117	**What is Friar Laurence's state of mind – calm, nervous or uneasy?**
	Friar Laurence is very uneasy.
p. 118	**What does Juliet complain about?**
	Juliet feels frustrated because Romeo has drained his cup to the dregs, thereby preventing her from committing suicide by poisoning herself.
p. 120	**Why does he say "newly dead"?**
	The adverb *newly* has a double meaning here: (1) 'recently', and (2) 'anew'. The blood trickling from the wound in Juliet's breast attests the recency of her death, and she seems to have died a second time because she appeared to be dead when she was interred.
p. 120	**Shakespeare has used the word 'ground' twice. Why?**
	The repetition of the word *ground* can be explained by Shakespeare's marked predilection for punning. In the first main clause *ground* means 'earth', but in the second main clause it means 'reason'.
p. 120	**Where else did the Prince appear on the stage? Do you see any dramatic connection?**
	The Prince also appears in Act 1, Scene 1, in the midst of a fierce affray between the Capulets and the Montagues, and in Act 3, Scene 1, just after the brawl in which Mercutio and Tybalt perish. In Act 1, Scene 1, the Prince, who represents law and order, calls for an end to violence and manages to stop the fighting, but in Act 3, Scene 1 and Act 5, Scene 3 he arrives too late to prevent a tragedy.
p. 121	**What sad news is conveyed to the Prince?**
	Montague tells the Prince that his wife died of grief on learning that her son had been banished.
p. 121	**Who does the Friar address when he says 'you'?**
	At this point the Friar addresses Lord Capulet.
p. 122	**Is Friar Laurence's long explanation of the events dramatically necessary?**
	Strictly speaking, Friar Laurence's explanations are unnecessary since the audience is already acquainted with the facts he reports. The surviving protagonists, however, need to be informed of the events which led to the tragic deaths of the lovers.

From whose letter does the Prince quote? ◀ p. 123

The Prince quotes from a letter which Romeo gave to Balthasar before entering the Capulets' tomb.

Activities

The children of two renowned families are buried. The requiem mass is celebrated by Friar Laurence, who has vowed to preach a sermon that the two guilty families will not forget.

◀ Preaching an unforgettable sermon p. 124

1. Write this sermon.

My dear brethren,

We have come together to bury two unhappy young lovers who would still be alive today if the Capulets and the Montagues had ended their long-standing feud before matters got out of hand.

The inveterate hostility between the two families has caused much needless suffering. Need I remind you how Mercutio met a violent death at Tybalt's hands, Tybalt and Paris were slain by Romeo, Romeo and Juliet, driven to despair, ended their lives in the fearful gloom of a burial vault, and Lady Montague – alas! – died of grief on learning of her son's banishment?

Blinded by arrogance and an insatiable thirst for revenge, the Capulets and the Montagues heeded neither the warnings of our Prince nor the precepts of the holy Church; and they were too preoccupied with their futile quarrels to notice that their children had fallen in love with each other. Their guilt is manifest, and on the Day of Judgement they will be held responsible for the tragic chain of events leading to the deaths which we now mourn.

The bodies of Romeo and Juliet now lie rotting in the summer heat. But where are their souls? Are they in heaven, or are they in hell? Let us hope that God in His infinite mercy will save them from eternal damnation and forgive their parents for their dreadful sins. Amen.

2. Make a video or tape recording of the best sermon.

Special attention should be given to clear diction and stylistic elegance.

3. The Nurse and Benvolio meet in front of the cathedral as they are both about to attend the requiem. What will they talk about?

They will probably talk about two main topics: (1) the tragic events that occurred at the cemetery, and (2) the reconciliation between the Capulets and Montagues.

In Act 1, Scene 1 Lady Montague tries to keep her husband from mingling in the street fight with the Capulets. As a close friend of the family, you have lived with them through all their ups and downs. You vividly remember Lady Montague's last days before she died. Write an epitaph of eight lines for her gravestone. You can work in groups.

◀ Remembering a beloved person p. 124

Lady Montague's epitaph might read as follows:

Here lies a noble lady, renowned for her grace, her modesty and her steadfastness. She was a dutiful wife, a loving mother, a devout Christian. Her life was hard, her death untimely. She lived in fear and died of grief. Her inconsolable husband has erected this stone, a monument to her virtues and his love.

Heaven or hell? ▶
p. 124

Romeo and Juliet have committed suicide – an act condemned by Islam, Judaism and Christianity. Start an interdisciplinary discussion with your English and religious education teacher and try to answer the question, if Romeo and Juliet are eternally lost or saved by the Grace of God.

A devout Christian might put forward the following arguments and counterarguments:
- From the earliest days Christian leaders have condemned suicide, so there seems little doubt that Romeo and Juliet richly deserve everlasting damnation.
- The traditional catalogue of the seven deadly sins is: (1) vainglory; (2) covetousness; (3) lust; (4) envy; (5) gluttony; (6) anger; and (7) sloth. Since suicide does not appear in this catalogue, there seems little reason to asume that Romeo and Juliet will suffer eternal damnation.
- Since God is merciful, there are good grounds for believing that the lovers will be saved from eternal damnation.

An atheist, by contrast, might say that there is no point in discussing the afterlife since there is insufficient evidence to prove that life continues after death.

Reviewing Act Five

Adding a scene of ▶
your own
p. 124

Write a new scene – scene 4 – in which the Prince calls everybody involved in these "civil brawls" to appear in court in order to administer justice.

1. Who do you think he will summon?

There can be no doubt that he will summon Capulet and Montague.

2. What charges will he bring against them?

They will be charged with inciting their followers to violence and causing serious disturbances.

3. Write this scene, then make a video production of it. If possible, put the script on your homepage on the Internet and ask Internet surfers to comment on your results.

The scene might be constructed along the following lines:

Prince: Although I have expressly forbidden violent behaviour in public places, our fair city has been torn for many years by civil strife. The time has now come when those responsible for this deplorable state of affairs must be brought to justice. Capulet and Montague, I hereby charge you with multiple breaches of the peace which have resulted in the deaths of several innocent people, including two of my own kinsmen. What have you to say for yourself, Capulet?

Capulet: Prince, I have no choice but to plead guilty. By inciting my followers to violence I have caused serious disturbances in the streets. I humbly beg forgiveness for my misdeeds.

Prince: And what have you to say for yourself, Montague?

Montague: Prince, I plead guilty, too. I have kindled civil strife, and I am willing to make amends for all the offences I have committed.

Prince: I could banish you, or even sentence both of you to death, but I shall temper justice with mercy since Fate has already punished you most cruelly by depriving you of your beloved children.

Capulet and Montague: Thank you, Prince.

Prince: I shall merely sentence you to a heavy fine if you will make a solemn pledge … You must make peace with each other, and you must never again incite your followers to violence of any kind. Capulet, give your hand to Montague.

Capulet (*reaching out his hand*): Most willingly, Prince. I yield to your request.

Montague (*taking Capulet's hand in his*): Prince, we shall observe your laws and heal our chronic feud. I solemnly promise to keep the peace.

Capulet: And so do I, Prince.

Hand in hand, Capulet and Montague stand with bowed heads before the Prince.

Compare the Romeo you know from Act One with the Romeo of this last act.

◀ **Young man of great character p. 125**

1. Has he matured or not? Discuss.

Throughout the play, Romeo is portrayed as an extremely immature young man. The following arguments could be put forward in support of the thesis that Romeo remains immature from beginning to end:

- In the first act Romeo is merely a conventional lover in the sonnet tradition – a lovesick swain pining for a girl called Rosaline. His solemn vapourings about unrequited love are absurdly boyish.
- In the window scene (Act 2, Scene 2) he appears much less prudent and realistic than Juliet. His passion for Juliet makes him blind to everything else.
- His immaturity is revealed once more in Act 3, Scene 3, where Friar Laurence tells him he has been banished. Consumed with self-pity, Romeo rolls on the ground, weeping hysterically and lamenting his fate, and he even tries to stab himself when the Nurse describes Juliet's grief.
- His decision to commit suicide in the Capulets' tomb shows his inability to control his emotions.

Despite the brief time-spread of the play, there are, however, a few signs of maturation:

- At the beginning of Act 2, Scene 6 he speaks of his feelings for Juliet in terms which show that in spite of his youthful impetuosity he has already outgrown his risible unrequited passion for Rosaline and achieved a remarkably mature understanding of love.
- In the final act the report of Juliet's death fails to produce a repetition of the emotional self-indulgence of Act 3, Scene 3. Instead of wallowing in self-pity, Romeo receives the news with control, quiet resolution and unhesitating commitment: 'Well, Juliet, I will lie with thee tonight.'

2. Would you have decided to end your life because your girlfriend had done so? Explain your decision.

A student who has suicidal tendencies might answer this question as follows:

I've a girlfriend who means everything to me. If she were to commit suicide I'd have no purpose in life, so I'd probably kill myself, too.

By contrast, a young man with a more positive attitude to life might write something like this:

I've a very nice girlfriend and I'd be terribly sad if she were to kill herself, but I'd never contemplate suicide. I suppose it would take me time to get over the shock, but after a few months I'd start looking for a new girlfriend.

Friends or foes? ▶ p. 125

Balthasar and Paris's pages meet after attending the funeral mass.

1. What will they talk about?

They will probably talk about the tragic turn of events that led to the murder of Paris and the suicide of Romeo and Juliet.

2. How will they behave towards each other?

There may be some awkwardness between them since their masters were rivals.

Linguistic simplicity? ▶ p. 125

Friar Laurence's choice of words has often been very complex. Why do you think his last speech is much simpler to understand?

In his final speech, Friar Laurence puts aside all rhetoric because he is confused and deeply distressed.

Vox populi! ▶ p. 125

Imagine you are just about to go shopping when this "open outcry" of the people comes to your attention.

1. How would you react to this public tumult?

I would probably follow the crowd out of curiosity.

2. Which party might you side with? Give reasons for your decision.

If there was an argument between the Capulets and the Montagues in front of the Capulets' tomb, I would probably side with the Montagues because they seem more likeable and more respectable than the Capulets.

Reviewing the play

1. Is Harold Bloom right in his view that Mercutio is a 'scene stealer'?

◀ Exit a rival? p. 125

In this discussion the teacher should draw the students' attention to the following points:
a. Mercutio is the 'scene stealer' insofar as he is the hot-blooded Italian male full of pugnacity although he attributes this characteristic trait to Benvolio (cf. Act 3, scene 1, ll. 15–28).
b. In spite of his uncle's orders not to quarrel, he sides with Romeo and roams the streets in order to pick a fight with Romeo's enemies. The feud is quite clearly a mere pretext to him; he is a trouble maker.
c. If Mercutio had succeeded in killing Tybalt, the whole action would have ended differently; so a concentration on Romeo's and Juliet's relationship could only be successful from a dramatic point of view if Mercutio vanished from the scene.

2. Which characteristic traits did you like / dislike in Mercutio?

Shakespeare makes use of Mercutio as a kind of foil to Romeo but only as long as Romeo is in search of his true love. As soon as Romeo meets Juliet, Mercutio stops teasing Romeo about being in love, as it seems, with Rosaline, as his role as a jester and merry maker is no longer needed.
So, what do we like or dislike in Mercutio? Let's sum up his positive as well as negative qualities:

Positive	Negative
He is lively, cracking jokes, sometimes carrying it too far; he is a real friend, witty and energetic.	His language is very colloquial, often bordering on the obscene; he does not know what true love means; instead he mistakes sex for love; sometimes he can be very quarrelsome.

3. Would you have given Mercutio a longer 'life' on the stage if you had been the author of the play? Give reasons for your decision.

A longer 'life' on the stage would obviously change the whole course of the drama. It might be interesting to hear what plausible suggestions the students offer in order to 'prolong' Mercutio's life on the stage or if they support his early exit.

4. Film directors sometimes detect a certain homoerotic attraction in the relationship between Romeo and Mercutio. In your view, is there any hint in the text that could support this interpretation?

According to Harold Bloom, whose book has been mentioned above, *Romeo and Juliet* "is the largest and most persuasive celebration of romantic love in Western literature" (p. 90). It makes no reference to any passage in the *text* at all to homoeroticism. Some modern film directors have visually suggested a close relationship between Romeo and Mercutio. If Zeffirelli's film is shown to students, they will note that Mercutio's *Queen Mab* monologue ends with Romeo and Mercutio putting their heads together. Peter S. Donaldson interprets this moment as homoerotic: "Romeo's response – 'thou talk'st of nothing' – is transformed in the film from a reproach to an expression of compassion and concern, as the foreheads of the young men touch in an intimate two-shot."
(*Shakespearean Film / Shakespearean Directors,* Boston: Unwin Hyman, 1990, p. 158). A possible discussion of homosexuality in the play could start when this quotation is made known to the students.

5. Why has Shakespeare not dealt more closely with the relationship between Romeo and his mother?

Shakespeare often sides with the female members of his families and he certainly seems to sympathize with the females in this play. Nevertheless, there is only one passage in the whole play which tells us about Lady Montague's feelings towards her son. In Act 1, Scene 1 she expresses her satisfaction that Romeo "was not at this fray" (l. 111).

When the servants of the two houses fight in the market place, Montague wants to join the battle, but his wife scolds him: "Thou shalt not stir one foot to seek a foe" (l. 74). Bearing in mind that Romeo is never the first to start a quarrel, we can conclude that mother and son have one thing in common: neither is a trouble maker. But apart from that mother and son do not appear to have much in common. Shakespeare may have wanted to hint at a problem between parents and son, especially as we hear in Act 1, Scene 1 that Romeo has been seen "many a morning … with tears augmenting the fresh morning dew" (l. 125–126). His parents are aware of the fact that he seems somewhat depressed about something without knowing the reason for it.

So they ask Benvolio to find out what it is (l. 151). Either his parents do not care enough about his well-being or seem to find it difficult to communicate with him. Alternatively, Shakespeare is so preoccupied with the development of the relationship between Romeo and Juliet, that all other human problems are of minor importance to him.

A modern actress's point of view p. 126

1. Is Niamh Cusack right in saying that "Juliet has no relationship with her mother"?

a) Find passages in the text to support your answer.

Early in Act 1, scene 3 Lady Capulet seems reluctant to talk to her daughter in private although what she wants to discuss is a matter that should only concern mother and daughter. She can only talk about the question of marriage to Paris when the Nurse – out of the blue – mentions the possibility of marriage to Juliet: "And I might live to see thee married once" (l. 62).

Lady Capulet feels so relieved when hearing these words that she can now get down to business, i.e. asking her daughter what she thinks of getting married: "Thus then in brief, the valiant Paris seeks you for his love" (l. 74–75). This suggests that Lady Capulet has difficulties in communicating with her daughter, as it is hardly an indecent subject to talk about.

b) Then, bearing in mind that arranged marriages were normal at that time discuss whether the behaviour of Juliet's mother is reasonable or not.

Open discussion. The female participants of the course will probably have a lot to say about this question. Let's see what the outcome will be.

2. Can Juliet's situation be compared to Princess Diana's? Start a debate.

This may turn out to become a rather lively discussion, especially as we can say that these young women have one thing in common: they are left alone with their problems – then as well as now.

3. A teenager today being in Juliet's situation might simply use her mobile phone and ask her lover to elope with her to Gretna Green. Is that a solution to the complicated problem?

Such quick and rash decisions happen quite often, because these girls have not reflected on the consequences of their behaviour. We have heard that in such situations they may be disinherited by their fathers and that all bridges are burnt. Sometimes it may even be the beginning of an out-standing career of a young woman showing her will to be independent, but it can also end in complete misery – for all members of the family.

1. If we take Romeo's and Juliet's age into account, is the author right in stating that today's youngsters are "unfit" to read this play?
Start a debate by dividing the class into those who support the author's view and those who reject it.

◀ **Unfit for reading?**
p. 126

Peter Roberts has his students in New York in mind, who are, as a rule, younger than the students here in Germany when they read the play. So it will be interesting to hear what our students have to say about it.

2. To what extent do emotions, on the one hand, and the intellect, on the other hand, play a part in understanding Romeo's and Juliet's problems today?

Most readers of today will probably assert that they would never be ruled by emotions as much as Romeo was when he decided to take poison after hearing of Juliet's 'death'. Even at the moment of utmost grief most people say that reason would guide their action. But it is difficult to come to a decision because we very often do not act according to our ability to think but according to our feelings and these may be very intense at that moment when a beloved person – especially in his/her early life – has just died. It is easy to say that we are controlled by our intellect rather than by our emotions, but it may not always be true.

Your own likes and dislikes p. 127

And finally, express your own views about the play:
1. Which of these characters have your sympathies, which of them don't you like?

a) Montague

He is one of the minor characters. He speaks gently to his wife in Act 1, Scene 1 (152–153) although he behaves like a madman when he sees Capulet running into the market place in order to join the fight. He reappears at the end of the play and tells the Prince and the other characters on the stage that his wife has died (Act 5, Scene 3, ll. 210–211). He finally vows to erect a golden statue in memory of Juliet. At that point he appears fairly sympathetic.

b) Lady Montague

She only enters the stage twice; in Act 1, Scene 1 she speaks three lines (74 / 110–111); in Act 3, Scene 1 she is on stage but does not speak a word (ll. 136–138). Whether we like her or not is simply a matter of taste.

c) Prince Escalus

He is on the stage whenever something serious happens: In Act 1, Scene 1 he threatens the quarrelling houses with severe punishment (ll. 75–97); in Act 3, Scene 1 he mourns the death of his kinsman, Mercutio and banishes Romeo from Verona (ll. 178–193); in Act 5, Scene 3 he is informed by Friar Laurence about how the tragic denouement came about and finally tells the people that "some shall be pardoned and some punished (l. 308). He is powerful, but cannot prevent the Montagues and Capulets from starting riots in Verona's streets. All in all, however, he deserves our sympathies for trying to keep the peace.

d) The Nurse

She is the most equivocal character in the play. She is Juliet's companion as long as everything goes to plan but as soon as she has to take sides she clearly emerges as a woman without principles. So her unpredictable and fickle character makes her a highly dramatic figure on the stage but not a very trustworthy companion in the battle for allegiances and alliances.

e) Friar Laurence

He is a likeable but another ambiguous figure in the play. He helps Romeo to overcome his problems and tries to find a solution to Juliet's miserable situation. Although he joins the two youngsters in holy matrimony, believing that he can thus help end the hostilities between the two families, his plan fails because of an unforeseen accident: his letter to Romeo does not reach him, thereby triggering off the tragic denouement.

f) Paris

He is created by Shakespeare as a foil to the passionate and impetuous Romeo. Romeo asks Juliet to marry him whereas Paris asks her father first as the etiquette requires. He is a kinsman to the Prince and takes no part in the brawls in the market place. His courtship seems to be part of the formalities of that time; he is sincere but hardly an ardent lover.

In the final scene he convinces us that his love for Juliet is genuine. He fights Romeo because he thinks that young Montague has done "some villanous shame" (Act 5, Scene 3, l. 52) to Juliet and dies in the tomb of the Capulets. His fault is to love without being loved.

g) Lord and Lady Capulet

Shakespeare offers us more insight into Juliet's family and their problems than into those of the Montague family. Lady Capulet is much younger than her husband (about 26 years of age) and very close to Tybalt. Her lamentations after his death and her demand for Romeo's execution are understandable from her point of view. She knows her limits as Capulet's wife when she refuses to help Juliet. In other words, she would never endanger her marriage for Juliet's sake. She is not a born fighter for female rights and cannot be compared with Desdemona who simply marries Othello without telling her father.

Capulet has great affection for his daughter, but is, nevertheless, very angry when Juliet refuses to marry Paris. Neither he nor his wife know anything about the events of the previous two days.

As soon as they hear that their daughter has 'died' they are completely devastated. Whether Juliet's death finally brings the Capulets together, really does remain a blank, because it is not Shakespeare's business.

1. Baz Luhrmann, who made a film of the play in 1996, was quoted on the BBC as saying that "my adaptation of the play may be 'in' now, but will be forgotten in about ten years' time". – If you have seen this film, do you agree or disagree with him?

◄ **Film – helping the interpretation of the play?**
p. 127

During a film directors' symposium on 'Shakespeare in the cinema' Baz Luhrmann stressed that "one must simply address an audience at a particular moment in time" (Cineaste, Vol. XXIV, 1998, p. 53). The fact that his aggressive music at the beginning and the violence in parts of his film may reflect today's egoistic as well as vulnerable society can be conceded, but "the desperation with which it tries to 'update' the play and make it relevant is greatly depressing" (Roger Ebert, Chicago Sun-Times, 23 September 2000).

Fellow director, Franco Zeffirelli does not think highly of such "gimmikky cheesiness" – cf. Julian Lim, student's book, p.131 – when he states that "dressing character in modern costumes has (no) advantage … But apparently the pseudo-culture of young people today wouldn't have digested the play unless you dressed it up that way with all those fun and games" (Cineaste, ibid., p. 54).

Students should have ample opportunity to discuss the pros and cons of Luhrmann's film, especially in comparison with Zeffirelli's version of 1967.

2. Do you think a Shakespearean play should be accompanied in class by one or even two film versions
a) in order to understand an act or scene better?

When we make use of film versions of a Shakespearean play we should always remember that there are advantages as well as disadvantages of doing so. On the one hand, we will learn that "you're doing a great work by Shakespeare, but you're not prepared to include his language" (Trevor Nunn, *Cineaste,* ibid., p. 49). In other words, we will hardly find a film version that includes Shakespeare's words from the beginning to the end. As a result, we have to concentrate on excerpts that will help our students understand a particular scene because the film director may lay special emphasis on facial expressions and gestures which, understandably, cannot be found in the text. Take for example Act 1, Scene 5 as interpreted in the films by Zeffirelli, the BBC and Baz Luhrmann, which are all available for teaching. In the Zeffirelli version we not only hear Renaissance music and see Renaissance dancing, but are also shown Romeo's and Juliet's faces in close-ups when they see each other for the first time.

It is their fascination of getting to know a stranger that a film can express to an extent that even surpasses a stage performance, because close-ups are not available on the stage and because we can stop the film at a particular moment and use the still for our interpretation.

Although the BBC version is not highly acclaimed by critics, the way Capulet greets his guests and especially the masked faction of the Montague adherents helps us understand that the events that follow are much better than the words on the page can express. Baz Luhrmann makes the Capulet feast a celebration of a decadent high society which is so disgusting to Romeo that he has to put his head into a basin of cold water in order to cleanse himself morally. But what a sensation when he lifts up his face and sees Juliet standing behind an aquarium!

This close film analysis can be repeated with Act 2, Scene 2 or Act 3, Scene 5. Making use of films in the contemporary classroom is therefore a highly recommendable means to increase our students' motivation and to boost their creativity.

b) or should you only see a film after having finished the interpretation of the play?

A committed teacher who makes use of all the audio-visual aids available to him will not show a film when the 'work' is done. If we agree that the words of a play become alive through its dialogue and the characters' actions then audio-visual means should be employed at every stage of the interpretation, especially when the chance of students staging their own performance cannot be realized. Only 'studying' a play without any help of visual aids cannot be called a modern approach to drama teaching today. A film, seen at the end of an interpretation, is not a 'reward' for hard work just finished, as it was stressed in articles published in the 1960s or 70s in German periodicals. Film versions can open doors to the interpretation of a play much better than the simple discussion of the meaning of a certain word or sentence. In other words, in 2002 it is the method of teaching that has changed because of the technical means available to us. It would be wrong to make our students believe that we are living in the 21st century but want to go on teaching according to the methods valid in the 19th century.

Con-Texts

A Radio Discussion of Romeo and Juliet

Assignments

1. Are the two lovers "brought to ruin largely by the imbecility of their families" as Peter Ustinov says?

◀ p. 130

Ustinov modifies his assertion by adding the adverb *largely,* for he is evidently aware that the deaths of Romeo and Juliet are brought about by several circumstances: (1) the enmity between their parents, (2) the overmastering passion they feel for each other, and (3) a series of unfortunate events over which the protagonists have no control (Friar John's failure to deliver Friar Laurence's letter, Balthasar's journey to Mantua, and Friar Laurence's late arrival at the cemetery).

2. Are those critics right who put the blame on Romeo and Juliet themselves because they are irresponsible?

There seems little doubt that Romeo and Juliet are irresponsible, for they never consider the effects their actions might have on other people. Nonetheless, it would be unjust to lay all the blame on them, and several arguments might be put forward in their defence. First, they are very young and inexperienced. Secondly, the passion they feel for each other is so violent that it is like a blind and unpredictable force of nature. Thirdly, their tragic deaths are precipitated by circumstances entirely beyond their control.

3. Would you agree or disagree with Anna Calder-Marshall, who thinks that had the lovers decided to remain apart, "that would have been immaturity"? Discuss.

Calder-Marshall's conception of immaturity is very odd, to say the least. If Romeo and Juliet had decided to remain apart, they would have displayed the kind of stoicism that is the hallmark of Cornelian tragedy, and such stoicism has nothing whatever to do with immaturity. Romeo and Juliet get married because they are madly in love, not because they want to bring about a reconciliation between their parents.

A Review of Baz Luhrmann's Film Version of *Romeo and Juliet*

p. 132

> **Assignments**

1. Why is Shakespeare's *Romeo and Juliet* "the stuff rock'n'roll dreams are made on" and "ripe for … MTV treatment"?

In order to justify his assertion, Lim reminds us that Shakespeare's play is about a passionate love affair between teenagers – a relationship which sets them at loggerheads with their elders. The quotation under discussion might also be applied to Luhrmann's film because it is set in the second half of the twentieth century and accords great importance to American popular culture and the fantasy world of sex.

2. How does Luhrmann succeed in modernising Shakespeare's play?

In order to modernise Shakespeare's play, Luhrmann transfers the action from the late Middle Ages to the 1990s. The soundtrack is ultra-modern, the *dramatis personæ* wear fashionable clothes and smoke cigarettes, and we are shown hoardings where the merits of products like acne cream are advertised with the aid of quotations from Shakespeare's plays.

3. Julian Lim concentrates in his review on four characters: Mercutio, Tybalt, Romeo, and Juliet.
   a) What information are we given about them?
   b) What does he especially like or dislike concerning the two main characters?

a) Mercutio is presented as a psychotic drag queen with a predilection for psychedelic drugs; Tybalt is cast as a particularly dislikable character – a promiscuous homosexual who prides himself on his sexual prowess and who is bitterly jealous of Mercutio; Romeo is portrayed as a youthful lover driven by an elemental passion; and Juliet comes across as an innocent and vulnerable young girl endowed with courage and intelligence.

b) Lim dislikes DiCaprio's tendency to overact, but he has nothing but praise for Claire Danes' performance.

4. Julian Lim does not praise everything. What for example is he critical of?

There are five things that Lim objects to: (1) DiCaprio's tendency to overact, (2) the actors' clumsy handling of Shakespeare's language, (3) the way the soundtrack tends to divert the audience's attention from the text, (4) Luhrmann's failure to bring out the intense, tragic quality of Shakespeare's work, and (5) the fact that Luhrmann's production is sometimes too 'hip' to be convincing.

5. Language is a means of expressing oneself. How would you assess Julian Lim's style of writing in comparison with the one used by the participants voicing their opinions about *Romeo and Juliet* in Capitol Radio's discussion?

Since Lim and the Capitol Radio panelists had to operate in fundamentally different communicative situations, there are major stylistic differences between the two texts under discussion. These differences may be brought under the following heads: (a) speech versus writing, and (b) sobriety versus flamboyance.

(a) Speech versus Writing

The first text is a transcript of a radio discussion, whereas the second one is a film review that was published on the Internet. The predominant impression produced by the first text is one of conversational casualness. Although the panelists are highly articulate and manage to keep up an unbroken flow of speech, the informality of the conversational situation is maintained by a wide range of variety markers: contracted forms (e.g. *that's*), the adverbial intensifier *terribly*, the clarificatory phrase *I mean*, grammatical discontinuities (e.g. 'Star-crossed lovers – they're not really star-crossed at all'), redundancies ('have a close look at *Romeo and Juliet* in great detail'), and loose grammatical linkage of sentences (e.g. '*Romeo and Juliet* is the story of two young people who […] get married […] in secret. And it does need to be a secret […]').

The second text, by contrast, shows clear evidence of fairly complex advance planning. It exhibits a high degree of coherence. The arguments are presented logically, the paragraphs are tightly constructed, and the sentences are, on the whole, well built.

(b) Sobriety versus Flamboyance

By and large, the style employed by the Capitol Radio panelists is sober and straightforward. The contributions of Ustinov and McKellen reveal considerable skill in handling words, but Calder-Marshall's language is flat to the point of banality.

Lim, by contrast, writes with great gusto, and it is no exaggeration to say that his style is flamboyant. In the first text there is no straining after effects with unusual words and expressions, whereas the second text is seldom free from that kind of verbal affectation which is typical of the American popular press. Lim has a gift for ingenious phrasing, and he often jolts the English language out of its accustomed grooves in order to achieve expressiveness – witness the numerous nonce formations and unusual word combinations: 'on-first-sight', 'fast-cut', 'guns-blazing', 'Reservoir Dogs-style', 'gangster chic', 'matador-dancing grace', 'spaghetti western spoof', 'gimmicky cheesiness', 'inspired aptness', 'trippy mythworld'. Colloquialisms are also much in evidence: 'kids', 'folks', 'pulls this off', 'spoof', 'take' (used as a synonym of 'treatment'), 'shades of', 'cheesiness', 'hissy', 'stud', 'butch,' 'fem', 'guts', 'hip', and 'cheeky'. Mention should also be made of the word group 'the stuff rock'n'roll dreams are made on'. This is a witty allusion to one of Prospero's speeches in the fourth act of Shakespeare's *Tempest* ('We are such stuff / As dreams are made on').

There are, however, some interesting points of resemblance between Lim's article and the transcript of the radio discussion. Both texts contain examples of ternary sentence endings and elaborately balanced syntactic patterns:
- Text 1: 'a long, complicated and violent feud', 'fate, or chance, or perhaps just the feud?', '[…] a tragedy is merely a comedy that's gone wrong, just as a comedy is a tragedy that's gone right', '[…] youth versus age, love versus hate, life versus death'.
- Text 2: 'the fast-cut, guns-blazing, MTV treatment', 'elements of gangster chic, matador-dancing grace and spaghetti western spoof', 'irreverent, campy, and great fun', 'innocence and intelligence, vulnerability and exceptional guts'.

In Text 1 there is evidently a close correlation between the use of rhetorical tricks and the absence of hesitation phenomena, for a panel discussion is never entirely spontaneous. Similarly, in Text 2 we may establish a significant correlation between syntactic sophistication and other stylistic features such as the use of unusual word combinations.

Screenplay of *Romeo and Juliet*

Assignments

p. 139

1. This excerpt from the screenplay of Romeo and Juliet comprises the first 65 lines of Act 1, Scene 1.
   a) Work in groups: Find out which lines of Shakespeare's text have been left out.
   b) Having done so, would you say that Shakespeare's 'message' has been altered or twisted by the authors of the screenplay?

a) The following lines have been partially or totally omitted: 1–6, 8–10, 12–17, 27–28, 30, 31–33, 35–37, 56–57, 59, 65–66.

b) Luhrmann does not merely omit lines; he also makes numerous changes in the lines he retains. These modifications can be divided into two broad categories:

The modifications which fall into the first category are insignificant. Thus, for instance, the conjunction *but* has been inserted at the beginning of line 48, the position of *sir* has been modified in line 54, and the conjunction *and* has been put between the two imperatives in line 61.

By contrast, the changes that come within the second category are of prime importance:
- The most significant of these changes concerns the two servants who appear at the beginning of the film. In Shakespeare's play, Sampson and Gregory belong to the house of Capulet, whereas in Luhrmann's film they belong to the house of Montague. This fundamental

change entails a number of substitutions within the lines borrowed from the original text. Thus, in the first sentence spoken by Gregory in Luhrmann's film, the name *Capulet* has been substituted for *Montague*, 'maid of Montague's' (line 11) has been changed to 'maid of Capulets' (line 37), 'here comes of the house of Montagues' (lines 28–29) has been altered to 'Here comes of the House of Capulet' (line 71).

- As Sampson and Gregory now belong to the house of Montague, Benvolio, who is one of Romeo's friends, appears in their company at the beginning of the film. He is the driver of the pickup truck in which Sampson and Gregory travel along the freeway.
- Abraham (Abra), who in Shakespeare's play is a servant to Montague, is now presented as a servant to Capulet.
- Luhrmann introduces a new character, Petruchio, who is presented as Abra's sidekick.
- Since the brawl is started by Sampson and Gregory, we can no longer side with the Montagues, who seem to be no better than the Capulets.

This being so, there can be no doubt that Shakespeare's message has been radically altered.

2. Where is the opening scene of the film set? Does it change Shakespeare's intention of creating a certain atmosphere in any way? If so, to what extent?

The opening scene is set on a freeway which, if we are to believe the anchorwoman, is close to Verona. The information provided by the anchorwoman is, however, quite misleading since the action takes place in and around Verona Beach, a fictitious place somewhere in the United States.

By transferring the action to an ultra-modern setting in the 1990s, Luhrmann has completely changed the atmosphere of Shakespeare's play, thereby destroying much of the sombre charm engendered by the drama.

3. How does the appearance of the little boy (p. 136) add to the tension of the moment?

The dramatic tension is heightened by the appearance of the little boy because the child is particularly vulnerable.

4. Have a look at p. 138. There is a quick cut from one person to another or from one thing to another. How does this film technique affect the viewer?

The numerous cuts on p. 138 convey an impression of chaos and hectic movement, thereby creating a powerful dramatic effect.

5. Do you think Baz Luhrmann succeeds in giving new 'life' to an 'old' text? Discuss.

There can be no doubt that Luhrmann has succeeded in breathing new life into Shakespeare's text. From the artistic viewpoint, however, Luhrmann's action-packed film (produced in the USA and Mexico in

1996) is far from satisfactory because Shakespeare's work is essentially altered in spirit. Luhrmann's characters fail to move us as Shakespeare's do, and the archaic language of the original jars with the ultra-modern setting and the strident soundtrack.

Teil III

Klausurbeispiel

Petruchio's First Encounter With Katherina

Baptista
  Signor Petruchio, will you go with us,
  Or shall I send my daughter Kate to you?

Petruchio
  I pray you do. I'll attend her here – (...)
  Enter Katherina
  Good morrow, Kate, for that's your name, I hear.
Katherina
5   Well have you heard, but something hard of hearing –
  They call me Katherine that do talk of me.
Petruchio
  You lie, in faith, for you are called plain Kate,
  And bonny Kate, and sometimes Kate the curst.
  But Kate, the prettiest Kate in Christendom,
10 Kate of Kate-Hall, my super-dainty Kate –
  For dainties are all Kates – and therefore, Kate,
  Take this of me, Kate of my consolation:
  Hearing thy mildness praised in every town,
  Thy virtues spoke of and thy beauty sounded –
15 Yet not so deeply as to thee belongs –
  Myself am moved to woo thee for my wife.
Katherina
  'Moved' – in good time! Let him that moved you hither
  Remove you hence. I knew you at the first
  You were a movable.
Petruchio
20 Why, what's a movable?
Katherina
  A joint stool.
Petruchio
  Thou hast hit it. Come sit on me.
Katherina
  Asses are made to bear, and so are you.
Petruchio
  Women are made to bear, and so are you.
Katherina
25 No such jade as you, if me you mean.
Petruchio
  Alas, good Kate, I will not burden thee,
  For, knowing thee to be but young and light –
Katherina
  Too light for such a swain as you to catch,
  And yet as heavy as my weight should be.
Petruchio
30 'Should be'! Should – buzz!
Katherina
  Well tane, and like a buzzard.

William Shakespeare: The Taming of the Shrew, Act 2, Scene 1, ll. 162–164 / 178–202.

Annotations

8 **bonny** fair; **curst** malignant; shrewish; 10 **Kate-Hall** ironic form of address **super-dainty** very scrupulous or particular about something 11 **dainties … Kates** dainties, i.e. sweets were called 'cates' 14 **sounded** talked of; proclaimed 19 **movable** furniture / changeable person 20 **joint stool** wooden stool (used as an insult) 21 **bear** to carry loads 22 **bear** get children 23 **jade** very old horse / impotent man 24 **burden** accuse / make pregnant 25 **light** slender / promiscuous 26 swain bumpkin / foolish person 28 **should … buzz**: he puns on 'bee' **buzzard** a kind of hawk that cannot be trained and so: a foolish person doing everything only by chance **tane** taken

Assignments

1. Why is Petruchio eagerly looking forward to the encounter with Katherina? (Orientation / Context)

2. Shakespeare makes use of puns in this encounter between Katherina and Petruchio. Find examples in this excerpt and explain what their dramatic function is. (Analysis)

3. Choose one of the following tasks:
   a) Imagine a meeting between Romeo and Petruchio in which they discuss various ways to win a woman's heart. Invent a dialogue. (Evaluation)
   b) You are in love with a young woman / man called Juliet / Antonio. Write a poem or a letter in which you express your passionate love. (Re-creation of Text)

Solutions

1. The play "The Taming of the Shrew" is a comedy by William Shakespeare. As a matter-of-fact, it is a 'play-within-the play' that begins with a short introduction. A drunken tinker agrees to watch a play that is going to be performed for his benefit. The play that follows is set in Padua and deals with the hilarious battle between the sexes as Petruchio, a rich bachelor, is willing to marry the shrewish daughter of Signor Batista Minola, Katherina, simply because she is rich. Petruchio is therefore eager to meet Minola's shrewish daughter and this passage deals with this first meeting and the resulting conversation between the two of them.
The extract can be subdivided into four parts. In the first one (ll. 1–4) Petruchio sees Katherina for the very first time. When welcoming her he addresses her with a different name, calling her 'Kate' instead of Katherina which makes her, obviously, rather angry.
In the second part (ll. 5–15) Petruchio explains how she is described by others and how he sees her in contrast to other people's description.
In the third section (ll. 17–19) Katherina rejects Petruchio by telling him to leave her alone.
The last paragraph (ll. 20–29) deals with the banter between Petruchio and Katherina which turns out to be a battle of words with the intention to insult the other 'partner'.

2. The play 'The Taming of the Shrew' is filled with coarse, vivid and rough puns which enrich the 'conversation' between the two characters.

Shakespeare makes use of these puns in the very first encounter between Petruchio and Katherina. He does so in order to better convey the feelings both characters have for each other at first sight.

Petruchio starts the conversation with seemingly greeting Katherina in a very friendly way (l.4). Furthermore, he addresses her by calling her 'Kate' and explains his reason for doing so, saying that he has heard it before (l.4). This is a clever beginning because he makes her believe that he is reminded of her name at this very moment.

Katherina immediately takes up that casual remark by which he means to break the ice. She, however, twists his words by answering him that he is 'hard of hearing' (l. 5). This insult implying that Petruchio is 'deaf', sets her tone for the conversation to follow from the very beginning. Apart from that, she corrects him by stating that "they call me Katherina that do talk of me" (l.6).

But Petruchio does not let himself be put off by her reply and states that she is lying about her name (l. 7). He makes fun of her by enumerating her advantages she has according to what people say and what he thinks of her himself. He tells Katherina that other persons think of her as 'plain' (l. 7), 'bonny' (l.8) and 'curst' (l. 8). But at the same time he says what he thinks of her and praises her by playing with words as was the custom at Shakespeare's time.

He ironically calls her 'Kate-Hall' (l. 10) and describes her as 'super-dainty' (l. 10), which implies that she is very scrupulous. At the same time he uses the second meaning of the word 'dainty' in order to pay her a compliment. He uses a pun when saying that "dainties are all Kates" (l. 11). With the word 'Kates' he thinks, on the one hand, of women having this name and on the other hand, of sweets which are also called like that but are written in a slightly different way.

He continues to praise Katherina and, finally, he reveals to her the reason for all those compliments. He is "moved to woo (her) for (his) wife (l.16). He seems to think that the sharp contrast between his opinion of her and other people's opinion in addition to his witty compliments are enough reasons for her to agree to the marriage proposal.

But Katherina is indifferent to and unimpressed by those compliments. Moreover, she once again flings his words back at him by using a pun. She tells him, in a very straightforward way, to go back where he comes from: "Let him that moved you hither remove you hence" (ll. 17–18). That statement implies that Katherina suspects Petruchio to be sent by someone else. Because of his straightforward marriage proposal and the fact that her sister is not allowed to marry before her, Katherina's conclusion seems plausible.

She underlines her suspicions by calling him "a movable" (l. 19). She has apparently seen through his plan and calls him on it.

Petruchio tries not to show that his plan has failed and innocently asks her: "What's a movable?" (l.19). She replies rather snippily that it is "a joint stool" (l. 20).

Petruchio takes up this punning challenge and goes even a step further by telling her that she has "hit it" (l. 20) and quickly invites her: "Come sit on me" (l. 20). He has apparently noticed that he will not achieve anything by trying to flatter her. Therefore he tries a different tactic and plays along with her rough replies.

Katherina is not impressed and continues to torment him by once again taking up his reply, turning it into an insult: "Asses are made to bear, and so are you" (l. 21). Petruchio does not mind her making an ass of himself and, in a jiffy, counters her insult by playing on the word 'bear': "Women are made to bear, and so are you" (l. 22). With this statement he has the chance of returning to his marriage proposal: If she married him, she would have children, as this was one of the most important female duties to society at that time.

Nevertheless, Katherina is not willing to give in and bluntly proceeds with her attack: With a 'jade' like him it would be very difficult to have children at all. By calling him, very plainly, an impotent man, she must have hurt his feelings severely and told him that she is absolutely unwilling to marry him.

Therefore, he backs away from meeting her cruel words with equally harsh ones and returns to his first tactic. In regard to her accusation, he states that he has no intention of making her pregnant: "I will not burden thee" (l. 24). Furthermore, he once again praises her as being "young and light". This might look like a great compliment, but 'light' does not only mean 'slender', but can also mean 'promiscuous'.

Katherina quickly replies that she might be "too light for such a swain" as he would be "to catch" (l. 26). This statement shows that she seems to be completely satisfied with her current situation and lifestyle and does not need a foolish man trying to seduce her into marrying him.

The dialogue between the two characters shows the deep animosity Katherina feels towards Petruchio and his marriage proposal.

She tries to distance herself from the emotions evoked by his proposal by using harsh puns and giving insulting answers. By doing that she tries to stifle his feelings for her at the very beginning and to stop him from getting emotionally involved too much.

Petruchio, however, does not give up so easily and continues his word play as long as possible.

Shakespeare uses this huge amount of puns to let the reader / viewer enjoy this 'battle of words', thus giving fun to the audiences of his time and, at the same time, developing these two main characters.

3. My dear Juliet,

I take refuge to writing this letter in a last attempt to express the things I am not able to tell you. I will try to let you look into the innermost part of my heart in order to show you feelings that I myself did not know existed.

Juliet, I long for you, touch me, love me as I love you. I love you from the bottom of my heart; I never thought I could love anyone so completely as I love you.

For so long, I've wanted to tell you all these things hidden deep within my heart, my longings, my insecurities, my hopes.

But what holds me back from speaking to you is the suspicion that these feelings may not be returned. I hope and pray that you feel the way I do and that the moment will come when you will reveal your love for me.

At times, it's difficult for me to concentrate on anything other than my thoughts for you. In the weeks and months passed I tried to show my feelings through my behaviour towards you – each glance meant eternity to me, each touch of yours electrified me to the extent that I thought I would go crazy…

I find it more and more difficult to breathe as each passing moment consumes me. What a blessing it is to be consumed by you, by the intensity of your eyes and by the hidden treasures of your smile.

I am bound to you in ways you'll never know. I am yours with my body, mind and soul.

I am so utterly confident that, one day, you will share your feelings for me as I do now for the only woman I love – eternally, for you – Juliet.

Yours forever,
Antonio

Dieses ist eine leicht veränderte Fassung einer Schülerklausur, die von einer Schülerin des Kurses von Frau Illner, Schiller-Gymnasium Münster, geschrieben wurde. Der Herausgeber dieses LHB ist Frau Illner und ihrer Schülerin sehr dankbar für diese praktische Mithilfe.

Filmrezension

Zeffirelli's Romeo and Juliet (1968)
by Douglas Brodie

The major problem in translating drama to the screen has always been destroying the heavy-handed act divisions and singleness of locale which dominates most theatrical work. Shakespeare, by all means, should be the easiest dramatist to film successfully: he used the scene, not the act, as his basic unit for plot development and, considering the abrupt changes of locale and wide diversity of action, his plays bear far more resemblance to a film scenario than they do to a modern work of the theatre. Ironically enough the successful Shakespearean films are few and far between. But in 1968, Italian filmmaker Franco Zeffirelli offered a new version of Romeo and Juliet which sparkled as brightly as any Shakespeare has ever done on the screen. After the prologue was solemnly recited while travelogue shots set the scene, audiences were whisked into the marketplace, where the ancient feud is first seen on the level of pranks between the servants, leading up the social chain until the heads of both households are involved. Shakespeare could not have asked for more perfect visual metaphor for his perpetual theme as, in a matter of seconds, jokes turn into serious insults and a prank undergoes an unintentional metamorphosis into pure chaos in the public streets. Zeffirelli's cast was magnificent to behold. Pat Heywood, as the nurse, provided low comedy at its highest range of intelligence. Teenagers Leonard Whiting and Olivia Hussey didn't so much play Romeo and Juliet as they lived out the parts. Although each proved perfect in his role, Hussey was the standout of the two only because she looked to be precisely the right person for Juliet, while he was exactly the right type for Romeo. Whiting was natural, honest and never ruined the show trying to act; probably dozens of the other young men could have fared as well. Hussey, however, seemed irreplaceable; in the balcony scene her face changes in a matter of seconds from the innocent smile of a child to the mature stare of a woman. But rather than waste a great actor in the role of Romeo, Zeffirelli wisely saved his young talent for the part of Tybalt: Michael York brought the "prince of cats" to life, and his eyes burned with a brooding feline intensity and his ears actually seemed to be as pointed as Mr. Spock. Zeffirelli's most masterful touch came in his use of montage. Unlike so many modern moviemakers, who employed it promiscuously and continually in fear that their films might look either static or old fashioned, Z. reserved it for the proper moments. At the Capulets' dance the camera carries the viewer into the action with a pace which would have made even Richard Lester dizzy and double duels occupy a central place in the pacing of this picture not unlike the chase sequence in Bullit. But the film's appeal went beyond aesthetic quality. During the opening days of the decade Wise and Bernstein had re-interpreted S. for the early sixties by transplanting the star-crossed lovers to NY tenements in West Side Story; now, as the decade neared its end, Zeffirelli showed that R&J could prove equally relevant to the Free Love generation. Despite the exquisite period costumes, this 350-year-old tale appeared amazingly in tune with the current situation. Romeo in his first appearence is introduced as a flower child; Juliet as a naive teen who has not yet been radicalized against the insensitivity of the elders. Never before had actual teenagers been permitted to play the protagonists. But in an era when Hair had become the most successful show on Broadway, it made sense that R and J were at last depicted as teens who want to drop out of the establishment run by their parents. Their fight is with an unfeeling system and, by the end, they are destroyed by their idealistic actions. Zeffirelli clicked clearly not only because of his admirable artistic qualities, but also because he re-interpreted a time-honored tale in light of what was a happening to society in 1968.